# CAPITAL
# CELEBRATIONS

★

*U.S. Capitol at night.*

PUBLISHED BY THE JUNIOR LEAGUE OF WASHINGTON
Project coordinated by COOKBOOK COMMITTEE
Designed by MARTHA JO CHACONAS

Photography by DEAN ALEXANDER
Cover and all studio photography
copyright ©1997 by Dean Alexander

Food Styling by LISA CHERKASKY

Additional photography copyright © 1997:
©G. SILVERSTEIN, Washington Stock Photo Inc.: page 1. ©McGUIRE, Washington Stock Photo Inc.: pages 4 and 5.
©McGUIRE, Washington Stock Photo Inc.: page 7. ©G. PETROV, Washington Stock Photo Inc.: page 83.
©G. PETROV, Washington Stock Photo Inc.: page 129.

PRINTED IN THE UNITED STATES OF AMERICA
Favorite Recipes® Press
an imprint of

**FRP**™
1-800-358-0560
First Printing: 1997   30,000 copies

ISBN 0-9649444-1-3
Library of Congress Catalogue Number: 97-71678

# CAPITAL
# CELEBRATIONS

★

*A Collection of Recipes*

*by the*

*Junior League of Washington*

Photographs by Dean Alexander
Food Styling by Lisa Cherkasky
Design by Martha Jo Chaconas

Favorite Recipes® Press

# Table of Contents

★

*Springtime in Washington, D.C.*

## Introduction

IN THE EVER-CHANGING metropolitan community of Washington, D.C., people, administrations, and events come and go . . . but, for 85 years, the Junior League of Washington has stood firm in its commitment to address social challenges. ★ Today, the Junior League of Washington is an organization of 2,100 women devoted to promoting voluntarism, developing the potential for women, and improving communities through the effective action and leadership of trained volunteers. ★ The first project funded by the Junior League of Washington was a theater performance at Children's Hospital in 1913. Since that time, the League has raised millions of dollars, and has provided more than 250,000 hours of volunteer service annually. Vital community projects such as Bright Beginnings, a program for homeless preschool children, and the Higher Achievement Program, a tutoring program, work to educate and motivate disadvantaged youth. These are just two of the beneficiaries of numerous volunteer efforts. ★ *Capital Celebrations* is a companion book to the Junior League of Washington's successful *Capital Classics* cookbook. *Capital Celebrations* offers the best of the Washington region's recipes beautifully prepared with fresh ingredients. *Capital Celebrations* provides elegant recipes pleasing to the eye as well as to the palate that can be simply prepared by today's busy Washingtonians. ★ The Junior League of Washington invites you to enjoy these specially tested recipes and to celebrate the best of the exciting culinary tastes of our Nation's capital.

*JLW*

*Fourth of July celebration on the mall.*

"AN EMPTY STOMACH IS NOT A GOOD POLITICAL ADVISOR."

*Albert Einstein — Cosmic Religion*

# Appetizers

★

# Appetizers

★

Goat Cheese and Tomato Salsa Bruschetta.

# Goat Cheese and Tomato Salsa Bruschetta

*Simple yet sophisticated*

2 tomatoes, chopped and seeded
1 red pepper, chopped
1 yellow pepper, chopped
1 onion, chopped
2 tablespoons chopped fresh basil
2 tablespoons balsamic vinegar
2 tablespoons olive oil
1 French baguette
8 ounces Goat cheese, room temperature

Mix tomatoes, red and yellow peppers, onion, basil, vinegar and oil in a mixing bowl. Marinate for several minutes. Slice baguette into 1/2-inch thick rounds. Toast in a preheated 250 degree oven on a baking sheet until slightly brown. Cool. Spread with Goat cheese and top with a spoonful of tomato salsa.
*Yield: 20 servings*

★ *Salsa can be made several hours ahead.*

# Portobello Mushrooms in French Boule

*Contributed by William Jackson, Carlyle Grand Cafe*

3 ounces Portobello mushrooms
2 tablespoons olive oil, divided
1 tablespoon balsamic vinegar
   salt and pepper
1 (6 ounces) French boule
2 ounces Goat cheese
1/2 yellow pepper, grilled and peeled
1/2 red pepper, grilled and peeled
1 cup fresh baby spinach
1/2 lemon, juiced
   toothpicks

Combine mushrooms with 1 tablespoon of the olive oil and vinegar in a mixing bowl. Season with salt and pepper. Grill mushrooms until done. Season again with salt and pepper and chill. Slice boule in half and hollow centers out to allow for fillings. Spread bottom half of boule with Goat cheese, then layer with yellow and red peppers and grilled mushrooms. Toss spinach with the remaining 1 tablespoon of olive oil and lemon juice. Season with salt and pepper. Stuff top half of boule with spinach mixture. Place the 2 halves together and secure with toothpicks. Slice and serve.
*Yield: 1 sandwich*

## Tomato Tart with Olives and Cheeses

*Appealing presentation*

  1  (10-inch) prepared pie crust
  2  tomatoes
1¹/4 teaspoons salt, divided
  ¹/4  cup flour
  ¹/4  teaspoon freshly ground pepper
  2  tablespoons olive oil
  ¹/4  cup pitted Kalamata olives, sliced
  ³/4  cup minced green onions
  3  ounces Provolone cheese, thinly sliced
  2  eggs, beaten
  1  cup shredded Cheddar cheese
  1  cup heavy cream

Prick pie crust with a fork, and bake in a preheated 425 degree oven for 12 minutes. Set aside.

Slice each tomato into 4 slices. Sprinkle with ¹/2 teaspoon of the salt. Drain on paper towels, turning once, for 15 minutes. Combine flour, the remaining ³/4 teaspoon salt and pepper in a mixing bowl. Dip tomato slices in flour mixture. Sauté floured tomato slices briefly in olive oil in a skillet over medium-high heat. Be careful not to let tomato slices fall apart.

Line baked pie crust with olives, green onions and Provolone cheese. Top with cooked tomato slices. Combine eggs, Cheddar cheese and heavy cream in a mixing bowl. Pour over tomatoes. Bake in a preheated 375 degree oven for 45 minutes or until filling sets. Cool for 5 minutes before slicing. Serve warm or at room temperature. *Yield: 8 servings*

★ *This also serves 0 as a luncheon dish.*

## Chili Bacon Breadsticks

*Addictive*

15  slices bacon, room temperature
30  whole very thin breadsticks
  ¹/3  cup packed brown sugar
  2  tablespoons pure chili powder

Cut bacon lengthwise with kitchen scissors to make 30 slices. Stretch and wrap 1 bacon slice around each breadstick.

Combine brown sugar and chili powder in a shallow bowl large enough to accommodate the breadstick's length. Roll each bacon-wrapped breadstick in seasoning and place on a broiler rack.

Bake in a preheated 350 degree oven for 20 minutes. Loosen and let cool 15 minutes. Serve at room temperature. *Yield: 30 breadsticks*

## Mushroom Toast

  2  small onions, minced
12  ounces fresh mushrooms, thinly sliced
  3  to 4 tablespoons butter
1¹/2 cups freshly grated Parmesan cheese
1¹/2 to 1³/4 cups mayonnaise
  1  loaf party pumpernickel bread

Sauté onions and mushrooms in melted butter in a skillet until tender. Transfer to a mixing bowl. Add Parmesan cheese and mayonnaise, and mix well. The recipe may be prepared to this point and refrigerated.

Place slices of pumpernickel bread on an ungreased baking sheet, and top with mushroom mixture. Bake in a preheated 350 degree oven for 5 minutes; then broil for 1 minute or until mixture is brown and bubbly. *Yield: 24 to 30 servings*

# Pasta Fritters

*Different and delicious*

4 ounces capellini or spaghetti, cooked
3 green onions, finely chopped
3 tablespoons vegetable oil, divided
1/4 cup flour
2 tablespoons freshly grated Parmesan cheese
1/2 teaspoon salt
1/4 teaspoon pepper
1 egg
1/4 cup water

Coarsely chop cooked capellini or spaghetti, and set aside. Cook green onions in 1 tablespoon of the vegetable oil over medium heat, stirring occasionally, in a saucepan until green onions are tender and golden. Whisk flour, Parmesan cheese, salt, pepper, egg and water in a mixing bowl. Add cooked green onions and capellini or spaghetti. Mix until well combined.

Heat the remaining 2 tablespoons vegetable oil over medium heat in a nonstick skillet until oil is very hot. Drop batter by 1/2 cupfuls into the hot oil forming 4 mounds about 2 inches apart. Flatten fritter mounds slightly with a spatula. Cook fritters until golden brown on both sides. Drain on paper towels. Keep warm. Repeat with remaining batter.
*Yield: 8 fritters*

★ *Great way to use leftover capellini or spaghetti.*

# Bacon-Wrapped Stuffed Dates

*Sweet and savory*

8 bacon slices, halved
16 whole pitted dates
1/3 cup prepared scallion or chive cream cheese, softened
toothpicks

Partially cook bacon in batches over moderate heat in a skillet until soft. Drain on paper towels. Slice dates open on 1 side, and spoon about 1 teaspoon cream cheese into each date. Wrap with a partially-cooked bacon slice. Secure with toothpick. Broil dates for 2 minutes on each side or until browned. Cool dates slightly and serve warm.
*Yield: 16 hors d'oeuvres*

★ *This recipe can be doubled for a larger group.*

# Sun-Dried Tomato and Pesto Dip

2/3 cup chopped dehydrated sun-dried tomatoes
4 ounces of purchased pesto
1 cup plain nonfat yogurt
small fresh basil leaves for garnish

Plump tomatoes in water on High in microwave for 1 1/2 minutes in a microwave-safe bowl. Drain sun-dried tomatoes. Combine pesto, yogurt and sun-dried tomatoes in a serving bowl. Cover and chill. Garnish with basil leaves. Serve with favorite crackers.
*Yield: 2 cups*

# Baked Brie en Croûte with Mushrooms and Sage

*Truly elegant*

1 cup sliced wild mushrooms
1/4 cup loosely packed chopped fresh sage
1 tablespoon butter
1/4 cup dry Sherry
1 wheel (2 pounds) Brie cheese
1 sheet puff pastry
1/4 cup heavy cream

Sauté mushrooms and chopped sage in melted butter in a skillet. Add Sherry, and remove from heat. Remove top rind from Brie and set aside.

Roll puff pastry into a thin layer on a lightly floured surface until pastry is large enough to completely cover Brie. Spread cooked mushroom mixture in center of pastry. Place Brie, cut side down, on mushroom mixture. Moisten edges of pastry with water using a pastry brush. Gather corners of pastry to cover Brie completely.

Invert onto an ungreased baking sheet. Coat top and sides of pastry with heavy cream using a pastry brush. Make three slits in top of pastry. Bake in a preheated 425 degree oven for 20 minutes. Serve warm with crackers. *Yield: 12 to 16 servings*

# Warm Brie Cheese with Blueberry Chutney

*Delicious and beautiful*

1 cup fresh blueberries
2 tablespoons chopped onion
1 1/2 teaspoons grated fresh ginger
1/4 cup firmly packed brown sugar
2 tablespoons vinegar
1 1/2 teaspoons cornstarch
1/8 teaspoon salt
1 (3-inch) cinnamon stick
1 wheel (8 ounces) Brie cheese

Combine blueberries, onion, ginger, brown sugar, vinegar, cornstarch, salt and cinnamon stick in a saucepan. Mix well. Boil over medium heat, stirring frequently, for 1 minute. Remove cinnamon stick. Cover and refrigerate 30 to 45 minutes or until chutney is cold.

Bake Brie in an ovenproof serving dish in a preheated 350 degree oven for 5 minutes or until softened. Top warm Brie with cold chutney. Serve with crackers. *Yield: 15 servings*

★ *Blueberry chutney can be made up to 4 days ahead.*

# Brie with Roasted Garlic

*Your guests will rave*

- 2 heads whole garlic, unpeeled
- 1/4 cup olive oil
- 1 wheel (2 pounds) Brie cheese, chilled
- 1/2 cup Greek olives or ripe olives
- 4 teaspoons finely chopped fresh parsley

Cook garlic in olive oil over medium heat in a skillet, stirring occasionally, for 5 minutes. Reduce heat to medium-low. Cover and cook for an additional 15 minutes or until garlic is soft. Drain on paper towels.

Slice top rind off Brie. Place Brie, cut side up, on a baking sheet. Divide garlic into cloves and peel. Slice garlic cloves diagonally; do not sever completely. Pit and quarter olives. Arrange garlic fans and olives on top of Brie.

Bake, uncovered, in a preheated 400 degree oven for 10 to 12 minutes or until Brie is warm and slightly softened. Sprinkle with parsley. Serve with apple wedges, warm sourdough bread or French bread.
*Yield: 20 to 35 servings*

# Crawfish Dip

*Divinely zesty*

- 1 bunch fresh parsley, chopped
- 2 bunches green onions, chopped
- 1 cup butter
- 2 pounds crawfish tails
- 3 tablespoons garlic powder
- 32 ounces cream cheese
  salt and black pepper
  cayenne

Sauté parsley and green onions in butter over medium heat in a skillet. Rinse, drain, and coarsely chop crawfish. Add crawfish to skillet. Cook, stirring often, for 10 minutes. Add garlic powder and cream cheese. Lower heat and cook until the cream cheese is melted. Season with salt, pepper and cayenne, using twice as much of cayenne as black pepper. Serve with crackers. Dip can be frozen and reheated.
*Yield: 24 servings*

## Roasted Red Pepper Dip

*A delightful prelude*

1 1/2 cups roasted red peppers
  2 cups shredded Cheddar cheese
  2 cups shredded white Vermont Cheddar
    cheese
1 1/2 cups mayonnaise
  1 teaspoon hot sauce
1/2 cup minced leeks or green onions, white
    part only
  2 teaspoons freshly ground pepper
  1 teaspoon paprika
    crushed oregano
    basil
    thyme

Chop roasted red peppers and place in a mixing bowl with any leftover juices. Add Cheddar and Vermont Cheddar cheeses, mayonnaise, hot sauce, leeks or green onions, pepper and paprika. Season with oregano, basil and thyme. Cover. Refrigerate up to 3 days. *Yield: 5 to 6 cups*

★ *Also great for sandwiches.*

## Oyster Loaf

*Fabulous*

  1 loaf (1 pound) frozen bread dough
1/4 cup chopped celery
  1 cup chopped onion
  1 cup chopped green onions
  1 clove garlic, minced
  4 tablespoons melted butter, divided
  1 pint oysters in their liquid
1/4 teaspoon salt
    pinch of cayenne
  1 tablespoon flour
  1 tablespoon yellow cornmeal
1/2 cup shredded Mozzarella cheese
1/2 cup shredded American cheese
  1 tablespoon chopped pickled jalapeño pepper

Thaw and allow bread to rise according to package directions. Sauté celery, onion, green onions and garlic in 2 tablespoons of the butter over medium heat in a saucepan for 3 to 4 minutes or until vegetables are soft. Drain oysters, reserving liquid. Add oyster liquid to vegetables. Cook, stirring occasionally, for 3 to 4 additional minutes. Chop drained oysters, add to vegetables, and cook for 1 minute. Add salt and cayenne, mixing thoroughly, and simmer for 5 minutes.

Place risen dough on a surface sprinkled with flour and cornmeal. Slit loaf lengthwise halfway through thickness, then toward each side to create a pocket. Spread oyster mixture, Mozzarella and American cheeses and jalapeño peppers down the length of the dough pocket. Fold sides of dough over mixture, pinching to seal pocket. Brush top with the remaining 2 tablespoons melted butter. Bake in a 5x9-inch loaf pan in a preheated 375 degree oven for 25 to 30 minutes or until golden brown. Remove and cool for 2 minutes. Slice to serve. *Yield: 8 servings*

★

# Spring Rolls

*An Asian classic*

 1 clove garlic, minced
 2 slices fresh ginger, minced
1¹/2 tablespoons vegetable oil
 ¹/2 pound boneless pork, chicken or barbecue pork, shredded
1¹/2 cups fresh bean sprouts
 ¹/2 cup shredded bamboo shoots
 ¹/2 cup shredded carrots
 4 to 6 dried black mushrooms, soaked and shredded
 3 green onions, finely sliced
1¹/2 teaspoons garlic salt
 ¹/4 teaspoon five spice powder (optional)
 1 teaspoon sugar
 ¹/4 teaspoon pepper
 ¹/2 cup chicken broth, if needed
 4 tablespoons cold water, divided
 1 tablespoon cornstarch
 1 tablespoon flour
 1 pound egg roll wrappers, thawed in package
 4 cups vegetable oil

Heat garlic and ginger in vegetable oil over high heat in a wok. Add pork or chicken, and cook for 2 minutes. Add bean sprouts, bamboo shoots, carrots, mushrooms, green onions, garlic salt, five spice powder, sugar and pepper, and cook for an additional 2 minutes. Moisten with chicken broth, if needed. Stir 2 tablespoons of the cold water together with cornstarch in a mixing bowl. Add cornstarch mixture to wok, and cook for 1 minute. Remove wok from heat. Combine flour with the remaining 2 tablespoons water in a small bowl to create a paste and set aside.

Take one egg roll wrapper at a time from package, and cover remaining wrappers with a slightly damp paper towel. Place about 2¹/2 tablespoons filling in the center of egg roll wrapper. Roll in egg roll fashion and seal with flour paste.

Fry spring rolls in hot vegetable oil in a skillet until lightly browned and floating in the oil. Drain on paper towels. To reheat, place in a preheated 350 degree oven for 12 to 14 minutes. Serve with Chinese hot mustard and duck or plum sauce.

*Yield: 16 servings*

★ *You may replace the bean sprouts with Napa cabbage. Spring rolls may be assembled ahead and frozen until ready to serve. When ready to serve, thaw, and fry as described above.*

# Fried Wonton Envelopes

*A crowd pleaser*

- 8 ounces Cheddar cheese
- 24 small wonton wrappers
  vegetable cooking spray
  vegetable oil

Cut cheese into 1x1x1/2-inch pieces. Place one piece of cheese in the center of each wonton wrapper. Moisten edges of wrapper with water. Fold corners of wrapper to the center, overlapping edges slightly to enclose cheese filling. Place wonton packages on wax paper sprayed with vegetable cooking spray. Cover with additional wax paper to prevent the wontons from drying out.

Pour 3 inches of vegetable oil in a deep skillet and heat to 350 degrees. Fry 4 to 6 wontons at a time, turning over once, until golden brown on each side. Drain on paper towels. Serve immediately.
*Yield: 24 servings*

★ *Good alone or dipped in tomato sauce, guacamole dip or sweet and sour sauce. Experiment with different cheeses such as Swiss, Monterey Jack or Gouda.*

# Meatballs in Cranberry Sauce

*A pleasant departure from the usual meatball*

- 1 pound ground beef or sausage
- 1 egg, beaten
- 3/4 cup soft bread crumbs
- 2 tablespoons finely chopped onion
- 1 clove garlic, minced
- 2 tablespoons catsup
- 1 tablespoon minced fresh parsley
- 1 can (8 ounces) whole cranberry sauce
- 1/2 cup thick and spicy barbecue sauce
- 2 jalapeño peppers, minced
  toothpicks

Combine ground beef or sausage, egg, bread crumbs, onion, garlic, catsup and parsley in a mixing bowl. Mix well. Form small (1 1/2-inch) meatballs and place on a baking sheet. Bake in a preheated 350 degree oven for 15 minutes or until cooked through, turning the meatballs once after 10 minutes to brown. Drain on paper towels.

Combine cranberry sauce, barbecue sauce and jalapeño peppers in a saucepan. Heat until sauce is boiling. Combine cooked meatballs and cranberry sauce in a chafing dish. Serve with toothpicks.
*Yield: 48 meatballs*

★ *The meatballs can be made in advance, and either refrigerated or frozen. Cooked cheese tortellini may be added to the meatballs for variety.*

# Chili Verde Cheese Puffs

1/2 cup butter
1 cup water
1 cup flour
1 teaspoon salt
4 eggs
8 ounces cream cheese, softened
4 ounces chopped mild green chilies, drained

Heat butter and water in a saucepan until boiling. Add flour and salt. Reduce heat to low and continue cooking, stirring constantly, for 3 minutes. Place mixture in a food processor with a steel blade. Add eggs, 1 at a time, with motor running. Process until dough appears satiny. Drop teaspoonfuls of dough onto an ungreased baking sheet. Bake in a preheated 375 degree oven for 15 minutes. After 13 minutes, insert a knife tip into each puff and make a small incision about halfway down. Bake for an additional 2 minutes. Cool puffs on a wire rack.

Blend cream cheese in a food processor with a steel blade until smooth. Add green chilies and blend briefly. Slice puffs and fill with cream cheese mixture. Heat stuffed puffs on an ungreased baking sheet in a preheated 350 degree oven for 10 to 15 minutes or until hot. Serve immediately. *Yield: 48 puffs*

# Coconut Beer Shrimp

*Exotic and delicious*

1/2 pound unpeeled, raw large shrimp
1 cup flour, divided
1/2 teaspoon salt
1/4 teaspoon pepper
3/4 cup beer
1 cup flaked coconut, finely chopped
vegetable oil
scallion flower to garnish

Peel and devein shrimp, leaving tails on. Rinse well and set aside. Combine 1/4 cup of the flour, salt and pepper in a shallow bowl. Combine the remaining 3/4 cup flour and beer in a separate shallow bowl. Place coconut in another shallow bowl.

Heat 2 to 3 inches of vegetable oil in a heavy deep skillet to 350 degrees or until very hot. Dredge shrimp in flour, beer batter and coconut. Fry shrimp, 5 to 6 at a time, in hot oil for 45 seconds on each side or until golden brown. Drain on paper towels. Garnish with scallion flower. Serve immediately. *Yield: 4 to 6 servings*

★ *Serve alone or with a sweet and sour sauce. Also tasty with an orange sauce consisting of 1/4 cup orange marmalade combined with 2 tablespoons Dijon mustard.*

Coconut Beer Shrimp.

## Tangy Pork Tenderloin

*A buffet favorite*

 1 (1¹/2 to 2 pounds) pork tenderloin
¹/4 cup soy sauce
¹/4 cup sugar
1¹/2 teaspoons ground cinnamon
 2 tablespoons dry Sherry
 1 teaspoon ground ginger
 1 teaspoon dry mustard
 2 teaspoons fresh lemon juice
 2 teaspoons orange juice

Place pork tenderloin, soy sauce, sugar, cinnamon, Sherry, ginger, mustard, lemon juice and orange juice in a resealable plastic bag. Marinate for 6 hours or longer in refrigerator. Bake pork tenderloin in an ovenproof baking dish in a preheated 325 degree oven for 20 to 25 minutes or until the internal meat temperature reads 155 degrees. Baste frequently. Slice meat immediately and serve warm with small dinner rolls. *Yield: 16 servings*

## Fresh Appetizer Slices

*Pretty and elegant*

 2 packages refrigerated crescent dough
 8 ounces cream cheese, softened
¹/2 cup mayonnaise
¹/2 teaspoon dried oregano
 1 clove garlic, minced
¹/2 teaspoon freshly ground pepper
¹/2 cup crumbled Feta cheese
¹/4 cup pitted Kalamata olives, sliced
 2 tomatoes, seeded, drained and finely chopped
 3 green onions, finely chopped

Spread crescent dough, joining perforated seams, on an ungreased baking sheet. Roll sides up slightly. Bake in a preheated 375 degree oven for 10 to 12 minutes or until light brown. Cool.

Mix cream cheese, mayonnaise, oregano, garlic, pepper and Feta cheese in a mixing bowl until smooth. Spread over cooked crescent dough. Top with olives, tomatoes and green onions. Chill for ¹/2 hour to overnight. Slice into squares before serving.
*Yield: 45 servings*

★ *Low fat cream cheese and mayonnaise work great in this recipe.*

## Easy Boursin Cheese

*Great for a picnic on the Potomac*

16 ounces cream cheese, softened
 1 package garlic and herbs salad dressing mix
 4 tablespoons freshly grated Parmesan cheese
1/2 cup butter, softened
1/3 cup cracked peppercorns
1/3 cup chopped fresh parsley

Blend cream cheese, dressing mix, Parmesan cheese and butter in a food processor with a steel blade. Divide into two portions. Roll 1 portion in cracked peppercorns and the other in chopped parsley. Chill. Serve with crackers. *Yield: 2 small cheese rounds*

★ *Cheese can be served in an attractive bowl or crock, omitting parsley and peppercorns.*

## Cool-as-a-Cucumber Dip

*Great summertime dip*

 8 ounces cream cheese
 1 medium cucumber, peeled and chopped
1/4 cup chopped onion
1/2 teaspoon Worcestershire sauce
 1 teaspoon mayonnaise
   salt and pepper
   dash of Tabasco (optional)

Soften cream cheese in a mixing bowl in the microwave. Combine cucumber, onion, Worcestershire sauce and mayonnaise with softened cream cheese. Season with salt and pepper. Add Tabasco, if desired. Serve chilled with crackers. *Yield: 2 cups*

## Fresh Crudités with Thai Peanut Dip

*Even children love this dip*

 1 tablespoon minced shallots
3/4 teaspoon sesame oil
3/4 cup creamy peanut butter
1/4 cup lemon juice
1/4 cup soy sauce
1/2 cup water
 1 teaspoon red pepper flakes
 2 cloves garlic, crushed
 2 tablespoons shredded coconut
2 1/2 tablespoons brown sugar

Sauté shallots in sesame oil in a saucepan until transparent. Add peanut butter, lemon juice, soy sauce, water, red pepper flakes, garlic and shredded coconut. Cook, stirring constantly, over medium-low heat for 4 minutes. Add brown sugar. Cover and simmer, stirring frequently, for 10 minutes. If sauce thickens, add more water. Serve warm with fresh crudités. *Yield: 2 cups*

★ *Chunky peanut butter adds extra crunch.*

# Fabulous Fish Terrine

*Expensive but worth it*

---

parchment paper
butter
12 ounces fresh spinach leaves, washed
 4 to 5 sole fillets
1/2 tablespoon lemon juice
 1 pound salmon, boned and skinned
 2 egg whites
 6 tablespoons whipping cream
dash of Tabasco
salt and freshly ground pepper
 1 green onion or shallot, finely chopped
lemon twists to garnish
parsley or watercress to garnish
Fish Terrine Mayonnaise (recipe at right)

Butter a 5x9-inch loaf pan and line with parchment paper cut to fit bottom of pan. Butter parchment paper. Blanch spinach leaves. Squeeze dry, and finely chop. Wash sole fillets in lemon juice and cold water, and dry.

Line pan with sole crosswise and dark side up. Allow each piece of sole to hang over middle of the pan. Purée salmon, a little at a time, in a blender or food processor. Add egg whites, whipping cream and Tabasco. Season with salt and pepper. Add chopped green onion or shallot.

Spoon 1/2 of the salmon mixture over sole fillets. Layer 1/2 of the spinach over the salmon. Place remaining sole fillet lengthwise down pan. Spoon remaining spinach over sole fillet, and top with remaining salmon mixture. Tap pan on the counter to settle contents. Cover with overhanging pieces of sole. Cover with well-buttered parchment paper.

Set pan in another pan of hot water. Bake in a preheated 375 degree oven for 45 minutes or until skewer comes out clean. Carefully drain off liquid. Rest terrine in pan until cool. Refrigerate until ready to serve. Turn terrine out onto a serving platter. Garnish with lemon twists and fresh parsley or watercress. Ladle Fish Terrine Mayonnaise onto a plate, and place a slice of terrine on top.
*Yield: 12 to 15 servings*

★  *The recipe can be assembled hours before baking. The recipe can also serve 8 as a luncheon course.*

**Fish Terrine Mayonnaise**
 1 cup mayonnaise
 1 tablespoon Dijon mustard
 2 tablespoons dry Sherry
 2 to 3 spinach leaves
salt and pepper

Purée mayonnaise, mustard, Sherry and spinach leaves in a blender or food processor. Season with salt and pepper. Refrigerate until needed.
*Yield: 1 1/2 to 2 cups*

## Marinated Goat Cheese

*For the fennel lover*

  1  tablespoon fennel seeds, crushed
1½  teaspoons crushed red pepper flakes
  8  sprigs of fresh rosemary, plus extra
     for garnish
  1  cup olive oil
  1  teaspoon fresh lemon zest
  8  ounces mild Goat cheese
     fresh lemon zest for garnish

Combine fennel seeds, red pepper, rosemary sprigs, olive oil and lemon zest in a bowl. Pour over Goat cheese. Cover and marinate in refrigerator for 3 days or up to 3 weeks. Place cheese on a serving dish. Discard rosemary and lemon zest from marinade. Drizzle cheese with marinade. Garnish with fresh lemon zest and rosemary sprigs. Serve with water crackers. *Yield: 10 to 12 servings*

## Cheese Ball

*Georgetowners love this*

16  ounces cream cheese, softened
  4  ounces mango chutney
1½  cups raisins, chopped
½  teaspoon vanilla extract
¼  teaspoon curry powder
  1  teaspoon grated onion
½  cup chopped pecans or walnuts

Mix cream cheese, chutney, raisins, vanilla, curry powder and onion in a mixing bowl. Form mixture into a ball. Roll in pecans or walnuts. Chill overnight. Serve with crackers. *Yield: 12 to 10 servings*

## Spicy Black Bean and Corn Salsa

*Fun, fast and easy*

16  ounces canned black beans
16  ounces fresh or frozen corn kernels
½  cup chopped fresh cilantro
  2  jalapeño peppers, chopped
¼  cup chopped green onions
¼  cup chopped red onion
⅓  cup fresh lime juice
  3  tablespoons vegetable oil
  1  tablespoon ground cumin
     salt and freshly ground black pepper
  2  cups chopped ripe tomatoes, drained

Rinse and drain black beans well. Combine beans and corn in a bowl. Process cilantro, jalapeño peppers, green onions, red onion, lime juice, vegetable oil and cumin in a food processor or blender. Season with salt and pepper. Mix dressing with beans and corn. Cover and chill for 2 hours or overnight. Add tomatoes just before serving. Serve with blue and white tortilla chips. *Yield: 6 cups*

## Alii Nui Salsa

*Refreshing and different*

1 cup chopped fresh pineapple
1 cup chopped fresh mango
1 cup chopped fresh red pepper
2/3 cup finely chopped kiwifruit
1/2 cup finely chopped red onion
1/4 cup chopped fresh cilantro
1 tablespoon fresh lime juice
1 teaspoon minced serrano or jalapeño pepper
   salt and pepper

Combine the first 8 ingredients in a mixing bowl. Season with salt and pepper. Set aside for at least 2 hours. Serve with blue tortilla chips. *Yield: 12 servings*

★ *Add an additional teaspoon of jalapeño pepper for a spicier salsa.*

## Mexican Corn Dip

*Cool and delightful*

2 cans (11 ounces) Mexican corn, drained
4 ounces chopped green chilies
2 jalapeño peppers, chopped
5 green onions, chopped
1 tablespoon sugar
1 cup mayonnaise
1 cup sour cream
2 cups shredded sharp Cheddar cheese

Combine all the ingredients, mixing well, in a mixing bowl. Refrigerate overnight. Serve with tortilla chips. Keeps in the refrigerator for 5 days. *Yield: 16 servings*

## Party Starter Punch

2 quarts Champagne
1 quart Rhine wine
2 quarts soda water
1 pint lemon juice
1 cup superfine sugar
2 ounces Brandy
4 ounces orange liqueur

Combine all ingredients in a large punch bowl and serve. *Yield: 20 servings*

★ *Orange Curaçao, Triple Sec and Grand Marnier are different orange liqueurs that can be used in this punch.*

## Coffee Punch

*Perfect for a luncheon or shower*

1 cup sugar
8 cups strong coffee, hot
1 cup milk
1/2 gallon vanilla ice cream, cut into chunks
1 carton (8 ounces) frozen nondairy whipped topping

Add sugar to hot coffee, stir, and cool. Combine milk, ice cream and whipped topping gently in a separate mixing bowl. Ice cream and whipped topping should remain lumpy. Pour over cooled coffee and stir gently. Recipe can be prepared a day ahead, and refrigerated until serving. Serve in a large punch bowl. *Yield: 10 to 12 servings*

★ *One cup Vodka or Kahlúa can be added to serve as an after dinner dessert drink.*

# Brunch and Breads

★

# Brunch and Breads

★

*Florentine Egg Torte.*

# Florentine Egg Torte

*Elegant breakfast*

3 large shallots, chopped
7 tablespoons butter, divided
2 packages (10 ounces) frozen chopped spinach
2 egg whites, beaten
1 1/4 teaspoons salt, divided
1/4 teaspoon freshly grated nutmeg
   freshly ground pepper
3 slices firm white bread, crusts trimmed, torn into pieces
3 large green onions, cut into 1-inch pieces
1/2 cup chopped fresh parsley
1 cup milk
12 eggs
1/2 pound Swiss cheese, sliced, divided
3/4 pound lean sliced ham
3 red peppers, roasted and cut into quarters

Sauté shallots in 3 tablespoons of the butter in a skillet over medium heat for 5 minutes. Thaw and drain spinach. Combine shallots, spinach, egg whites, 1/2 teaspoon of the salt and nutmeg in a mixing bowl. Mix well. Season with freshly ground pepper. Set aside.

Process bread, green onions and fresh parsley in a food processor or blender for 5 seconds. Transfer to a separate mixing bowl. Add milk and soak for 5 minutes. Drain milk from the bread crumbs. Reserve drained milk in a separate mixing bowl.

Process eggs with 1/2 of the drained milk in a food processor for 10 seconds. Add reserved drained milk. Process until combined. Scramble eggs in the remaining 4 tablespoons melted butter over medium-high heat in a skillet until eggs are soft but not runny. Add the remaining 3/4 teaspoon salt and season with freshly ground pepper. Continue stirring eggs gently to prevent large, hard lumps forming.

While eggs are cooking, chop 1/4 pound of the Swiss cheese slices. Remove scrambled eggs from heat. Add soaked bread crumbs and chopped Swiss cheese, mixing thoroughly.

Smooth 1/2 of the scrambled eggs in a greased 9-inch springform pan with a spatula. Cover scrambled eggs with 1/2 of the spinach mixture, smoothing with spatula. Arrange sliced ham on spinach mixture. Arrange roasted red peppers over ham. Be sure roasted red peppers cover outer edge of the pan. Top roasted red peppers with the remaining spinach mixture, smoothing with spatula. Top with remaining scrambled eggs, smoothing with spatula. Layer the remaining sliced Swiss cheese on top. Cover base of springform pan with aluminum foil to catch any drippings. Recipe can be prepared a day in advance to this point and refrigerated.

Bring dish to room temperature before baking. Place filled springform pan on baking sheet to catch any liquid dripping from pan. Bake in a preheated 400 degree oven for 30 minutes. Remove from the oven. Rest for 10 minutes before unmolding. Drain off any excess liquid. Cut in wedges to serve.
*Yield: 8 to 10 servings*

★ *If roasted red peppers are not available, sauté 2 medium red peppers, julienne-cut, in 1 tablespoon butter until soft.*

# Spinach Sausage Brunch Casserole

*Serve to weekend guests*

1 pound bulk sweet Italian sausage
1 cup chopped onions
1 package (10 ounces) frozen chopped spinach
1 red pepper, chopped
1 cup shredded Mozzarella cheese
1 cup shredded Cheddar cheese
1 cup flour
1/2 cup freshly grated Parmesan cheese
1/2 teaspoon salt
8 eggs
2 cups milk

Brown sausage and onions in a skillet. Remove and drain grease. Thaw and drain spinach. Arrange cooked sausage in a greased 9x13-inch ovenproof baking dish. Sprinkle 1/2 of the red peppers over sausage. Top with spinach. Sprinkle spinach layer with Mozzarella and Cheddar cheeses and the remaining red peppers.

Combine flour, Parmesan cheese and salt in a mixing bowl. Combine eggs and milk in a separate mixing bowl, beating until smooth. Combine eggs with flour mixture until well blended. Pour filling over casserole.

Bake in a preheated 425 degree oven for 30 to 40 minutes or until knife inserted in center comes out clean. Let stand 5 minutes before serving. Cut into squares. *Yield: 8 to 10 servings*

# Country Club Breakfast

*Simple preparation*

10 slices white bread, cubed, divided
2 cups shredded Cheddar cheese
2 cups cubed ham
8 eggs, beaten
2 1/2 cups milk
1/2 teaspoon salt
1/2 teaspoon dry mustard
1/2 cup butter, melted

Line bottom of a greased 9x13-inch ovenproof baking dish with 3/4 of the bread cubes. Layer Cheddar cheese and ham over bread. Combine eggs, milk, salt and mustard in a mixing bowl. Pour over casserole. Top with the remaining bread. Pour melted butter over casserole. Refrigerate overnight. Bake in a preheated 350 degree oven for 1 hour.
*Yield: 8 servings*

# Farmer's Casserole

*A hearty breakfast*

    3 cups frozen shredded hash brown potatoes
  3/4 cup shredded Monterey Jack cheese with
      jalapeño peppers
    1 cup diced cooked ham
  1/4 cup chopped green onions
    4 eggs, beaten
    1 can (12 ounces) evaporated milk
  1/8 teaspoon salt
  1/4 teaspoon pepper

Grease a 2-quart square ovenproof baking dish. Spread hash brown potatoes evenly on the bottom, and sprinkle with Monterey Jack cheese, ham and green onions. Combine eggs, milk, salt and pepper in a mixing bowl. Pour over casserole. Cover and refrigerate 1 hour or overnight. Bake in a preheated 350 degree oven for 40 to 50 minutes.
*Yield: 4 to 6 servings*

★ *Uncooked casserole can be refrigerated, covered, up to 1 day and baked an additional 10 minutes.*

# Grits Casserole

*Down home cooking*

    1 quart milk
  1/2 cup butter
    1 teaspoon salt
    1 cup quick cooking grits
    4 ounces Monterey Jack Cheese with jalapeño
      peppers
      freshly grated Parmesan cheese to garnish

Bring milk to a boil. Add butter, salt and grits and cook, stirring often, until thick. Beat cooked grits with an electric mixer until fluffy. Pour grits into a greased 9x13-inch ovenproof baking dish. Slice Monterey Jack cheese into thin slices. Arrange on the cooked grits. Garnish with Parmesan cheese. Bake in a preheated 400 degree oven until cheese melts and looks toasty. *Yield: 6 to 8 servings*

★ *For a touch of elegance, substitute Gruyère cheese for Monterey Jack cheese.*

# Sausage in Puff Pastry

*A beautiful addition to brunch*

- 1  pound bulk pork sausage
- 1  medium onion, chopped
- 1  cup shredded Cheddar cheese
- 1  cup peeled, grated apple
- 1  package (17 ounces) frozen puff pastry, thawed
- 2  tablespoons milk

Brown sausage and onion over medium heat in a skillet, breaking sausage up well. Drain. Combine cooked sausage, Cheddar cheese and apple in a mixing bowl, mixing well. Set aside.

Roll one sheet of puff pastry out on a lightly floured surface to a 10x15-inch rectangle. Spread 1/2 of the sausage mixture lengthwise down the middle third of the pastry. Cutting from edges to sausage filling, cut left and right thirds into 1-inch wide strips. Fold alternating strips over filling in a crisscross pattern to look like a braid. Repeat with remaining puff pastry and sausage mixture.

Transfer pastry gently to a greased baking sheet. Brush top with milk. Bake in a preheated 400 degree oven for 25 to 30 minutes or until golden brown. *Yield: 12 servings*

★ *Recipe freezes well.*

# Blueberry Cheese Squares

- 1  cup flour
- 1  cup sugar, divided
- 1/4  teaspoon baking powder
- 1/2  teaspoon salt
- 1/4  cup half and half
- 1/4  cup butter, melted
- 1  egg, beaten
- 1 1/2  teaspoons vanilla extract, divided
- 2  eggs, beaten
- 2  cups fresh blueberries
- 1 1/4  cups Ricotta cheese
- 1 1/2  teaspoons cornstarch

Combine flour, 1/2 cup of the sugar, baking powder and salt in a mixing bowl. Add half and half, butter, 1 beaten egg and 1 teaspoon of the vanilla extract. Spoon batter evenly into a greased 9x9-inch baking pan. Sprinkle blueberries over batter.

Combine the remaining beaten eggs, Ricotta cheese, the remaining 1/2 cup sugar, cornstarch and the remaining 1/2 teaspoon vanilla in a mixing bowl until well blended. Spoon evenly over blueberries. Bake in a preheated 350 degree oven for 55 to 60 minutes or until knife inserted in center comes out clean. Cool. Cut into squares. *Yield: 9 servings*

# Strawberry Rhubarb Coffee Cake

*Delicious and unique treat*

2¹/4 cups flour
³/4 cup sugar
³/4 cup butter
1 teaspoon baking powder
¹/2 teaspoon baking soda
³/4 teaspoon ground cinnamon
¹/8 teaspoon salt
1 egg, beaten
1¹/2 teaspoons vanilla extract
³/4 cup buttermilk
vegetable cooking spray
1¹/2 cups Strawberry/Rhubarb Purée
(recipe at right)
confectioners' sugar (optional)

Combine flour and sugar in a mixing bowl. Cut butter in with a fork or pastry blender until mixture is crumbly. Set aside ¹/2 cup of flour/sugar mixture for topping.

Add baking powder, baking soda, cinnamon and salt to remaining flour/sugar mixture. Then add egg, vanilla and buttermilk to make a soft batter.

Spread ²/3 of the batter along bottom and side of a 9-inch springform pan coated with vegetable cooking spray. Spread Strawberry/Rhubarb Purée on top. Spoon or dollop remaining batter over the Strawberry/Rhubarb Purée layer. Pull tip of a knife gently through dough and Strawberry/Rhubarb Purée to lightly blend. Sprinkle reserved flour/sugar mixture on top.

Bake in a preheated 350 degree oven for 45 to 50 minutes or until cake tests done. Cool well. Dust with confectioners' sugar if desired.
*Yield: 8 to 10 servings*

**Strawberry/Rhubarb Purée**
2 cups rhubarb, diced into 1-inch cubes
1 cup sugar
2 cups fresh strawberries, hulled

Combine rhubarb and sugar in a mixing bowl. Let sit for 15 to 30 minutes until juices form. Add strawberries. Cook over medium heat in a saucepan, stirring occasionally, for 10 to 15 minutes or until fruit is dissolved and purée is smooth and thickened. Refrigerate until needed. Strawberry/Rhubarb Purée can be made up to 2 days ahead. *Yield: 1¹/2 to 2 cups*

★ *Use frozen rhubarb, if fresh rhubarb is not available.*

## Washington Waffles

*Fruit yogurt lends variety*

6 eggs, separated
1$^{1}/_{2}$ cups milk
1 cup butter, melted
1$^{1}/_{2}$ cups fruit flavored custard-style yogurt
3 cups flour
4 teaspoons baking powder
1 teaspoon baking soda
2 tablespoons sugar

Beat egg yolks in a mixing bowl. Blend in milk, melted butter and yogurt. Sift flour, baking powder, baking soda and sugar in a separate mixing bowl. Add to the yogurt mixture, beating well.

Whip egg whites in a mixing bowl until soft peaks form. Carefully fold beaten egg whites into batter until completely blended. Ladle batter into a hot waffle iron. Bake following manufacturer's directions. Serve waffles with syrup or fruit topping.
*Yield: 6 to 12 servings*

★ *Substitute 1$^{1}/_{2}$ cups sour cream for yogurt for a different taste.*

## Pecan Pancakes

*A special start to the day*

$^{1}/_{4}$ cup pecans, finely chopped
1 cup flour
1 tablespoon sugar
1 teaspoon baking powder
$^{1}/_{8}$ teaspoon salt
1 cup low fat milk
1 egg, beaten
2 tablespoons low fat plain yogurt
1 tablespoon butter, melted
   vegetable oil

Toast chopped pecans in a preheated 350 degree oven on a baking sheet for 2 minutes or until fragrant. Or cook pecans over medium heat in a heavy skillet, shaking the pan frequently, for 3 to 5 minutes or until fragrant.

Combine pecans, flour, sugar, baking powder and salt in a mixing bowl. Combine milk, egg and yogurt in a separate bowl, mixing until egg is well combined. Add to the dry ingredients using a spatula, or whisk until just mixed, adding melted butter in the process.

Heat griddle or skillet over medium high heat. Brush generously with vegetable oil. Griddle is ready when water sizzles on hot surface. Pour $^{1}/_{4}$ cup of batter on griddle at a time. Cook and flip pancakes after 2 to 3 minutes or when holes appear on top side and pancakes are brown on bottom. Cook until other side is brown. Set cooked pancakes aside on a warm plate until ready to serve. Repeat the process.
*Yield: 12 pancakes*

# Sticky Buns

*Well worth the effort*

1 package dry yeast
1/4 cup warm water
2 cups flour
2 tablespoons sugar
1/2 teaspoon salt
1/4 cup warm milk
1 egg, beaten
6 tablespoons melted butter, divided
2/3 cup packed brown sugar, divided
2 teaspoons ground cinnamon
1 tablespoon dark corn syrup
24 pecan halves
1/3 cup chopped pecans

Dissolve dry yeast in warm water. Combine yeast mixture, flour, sugar, salt, warm milk, beaten egg and 2 tablespoons of the melted butter in a mixing bowl. Knead dough for 10 minutes. Place in a greased mixing bowl. Cover and let rise for 1 to 1 1/2 hours in a warm, dry spot.

Combine 2 tablespoons of the melted butter, 1/3 cup of the brown sugar, 1 teaspoon of the cinnamon, and dark corn syrup in a mixing bowl. Spoon evenly into 6 large greased muffin cups. Place 4 pecan halves into each muffin cup.

Roll dough on a floured board to a 6x24-inch rectangle. Brush with remaining 2 tablespoons melted butter. Combine the remaining 1/3 cup brown sugar, the remaining 1 teaspoon cinnamon and chopped pecans in a mixing bowl. Sprinkle over dough. At 6-inch side, roll dough up tightly. Slice into six 1-inch rounds.

Place sliced dough in muffin cups cut side down. Press lightly in the center. Cover filled muffin cups. Let dough rise for 20 to 30 minutes. If center rises higher than sides of muffin cups, press dough lightly until even. Bake in a preheated 375 degree oven for 25 to 30 minutes or until brown. Remove. Let rest for 1 minute. Loosen sides of sticky buns. Carefully invert onto a serving dish. Serve warm.
*Yield: 6 servings*

Sticky Buns.

# Sour Cream Coffee Cake

*An all-occasion favorite*

   1 cup unsalted butter, softened
2 3/4 cups sugar, divided
   2 eggs, beaten
   2 cups sour cream
   1 tablespoon vanilla extract
   2 cups flour
   1 tablespoon baking powder
1/4 teaspoon salt
   2 cups chopped pecans
   1 tablespoon ground cinnamon

Cream butter and 2 cups of the sugar together in a mixing bowl. Add eggs, blending well. Add sour cream and vanilla. Sift flour, baking powder and salt in a separate mixing bowl. Fold dry ingredients into wet ingredients. Beat until batter is just blended. Combine pecans, cinnamon and the remaining 3/4 cup sugar in a separate mixing bowl.

Pour 1/2 of the batter into a greased and floured 10-inch bundt pan. Sprinkle with 1/2 of the pecan mixture. Add the remaining batter and top with the remaining pecan mixture. Bake in a preheated 350 degree oven for 1 hour. Serve warm.
*Yield: 10 to 12 servings*

★ *This recipe works great with low fat sour cream.*

# Maine Blueberry Cake

*A summertime favorite*

1/2 cup sugar
1/2 cup butter, softened
   2 eggs
2 1/2 cups flour
   1 teaspoon baking powder
1/2 teaspoon baking soda
1/8 teaspoon salt
1/2 cup buttermilk
   1 teaspoon vanilla extract
   2 cups fresh blueberries
   4 tablespoons butter, melted
   1 teaspoon cinnamon sugar

Cream sugar and butter together in a mixing bowl until light and fluffy. Add eggs. Combine flour, baking powder, baking soda and salt together in a separate mixing bowl. Add flour mixture to sugar mixture alternating with buttermilk and vanilla. Fold in blueberries. Pour batter into a greased 8-inch square pan. Pour melted butter over batter. Sprinkle with cinnamon sugar. Bake in a preheated 350 degree oven for 30 to 35 minutes. *Yield: 6 to 8 servings*

★ *To make cinnamon sugar, combine 1/2 teaspoon sugar and 1/2 teaspoon cinnamon.*

# Exotic Oat Bran Muffins
# with Ginger Butter

*Ginger butter adds special taste*

   1  cup oat bran
   1  cup milk
1 1/2  cups mashed ripe bananas
 1/4  cup vegetable or peanut oil
   1  egg, beaten
1 1/2  cups flour
 1/3  cup packed brown sugar
 1/2  cup chopped walnuts or pecans
   2  teaspoons baking powder
 1/2  teaspoon baking soda
 1/2  teaspoon salt
      vegetable cooking spray
      Ginger Butter (recipe at right)

Combine oat bran and milk in a mixing bowl. Let stand for 3 minutes. Add mashed bananas, vegetable oil and egg. Mix flour, brown sugar, nuts, baking powder, baking soda and salt in a separate mixing bowl. Add bran and banana mixture to flour mixture, stirring just to moisten batter. Batter will be lumpy.

Fill greased muffin cups 3/4 full. Bake in a preheated 350 degree oven for 15 to 20 minutes or until the muffins are firm to touch and a toothpick inserted in centers come out clean. Cool on wire rack. Serve warm with Ginger Butter. *Yield: 12 muffins*

★ *This recipe will work with yellow, burro, red or manzano bananas.*

Ginger Butter
   1  cup unsalted butter
   2  tablespoons orange-blossom honey
   1  teaspoon finely grated fresh ginger
 1/4  teaspoon allspice

Cream ingredients together thoroughly in a food processor or a blender. Pack butter into a dish or a crock. Refrigerate until firm. *Yield: 1 cup*

# Tropical Fruit Bread

*A different quick bread*

3 cups flour
3 cups sugar
1 cup vegetable oil
1 cup milk
3 eggs
2 teaspoons baking soda
1 teaspoon salt
1/2 cup drained mandarin oranges
1/2 cup drained pineapple tidbits
1/2 cup mashed banana
1/4 cup shredded coconut
1 teaspoon vanilla extract
1/2 cup candied fruit or candied red cherries

Blend flour, sugar, vegetable oil, milk, eggs, baking soda and salt together in a mixing bowl with electric mixer on medium speed until smooth. Add mandarin oranges, pineapple, banana, coconut, vanilla and candied fruit or cherries. Continue mixing until smooth. Pour batter into 2 greased and floured 5x9-inch loaf pans. Bake in a preheated 350 degree oven for 45 minutes or until toothpick inserted in center comes out clean. Cool on a wire rack. Serve warm.
*Yield: 24 slices*

★ *Add 1/2 cup pecans or walnuts for variety. Frozen coconut works well.*

# Lemon Poppy Seed Muffins

*Moist and tangy*

3 cups flour
1 1/2 teaspoons baking soda
1 1/2 teaspoons baking powder
1/4 teaspoon salt
3/4 cup butter, softened
1 1/4 cups sugar
3 eggs
1 cup sour cream
1/3 cup lemon juice
1 1/2 teaspoons vanilla extract
3 tablespoons poppy seeds
1 1/2 teaspoons fresh lemon zest
sugar to garnish

Sift flour, baking soda, baking powder and salt in a mixing bowl. Set aside. Cream butter and sugar together in a separate mixing bowl until fluffy. Add eggs, 1 at a time, beating well each time. Combine sour cream, lemon juice and vanilla in a separate mixing bowl. Add flour mixture to butter/sugar mixture, alternating with sour cream mixture. Beat until well blended. Fold in poppy seeds and lemon zest. Fill greased muffin cups 2/3 full. Garnish with sugar. Bake in a preheated 375 degree oven for 18 to 20 minutes or until brown.
*Yield: 18 to 24 large muffins*

# Blueberry Orange Bread

2 tablespoons butter
1/4 cup boiling water
1 teaspoon fresh orange zest
1/2 cup orange juice
1 egg
1 1/2 cups sugar
2 cups flour
1 teaspoon salt
1 teaspoon baking powder
1/4 teaspoon baking soda
1 1/2 cups fresh blueberries

Melt butter in boiling water. Add orange zest and orange juice. Beat egg and sugar together in a mixing bowl until fluffy. Add to melted butter and water. Sift flour, salt, baking powder and baking soda in a mixing bowl. Add to the liquid ingredients. Fold in blueberries. Pour batter into a greased 5x9-inch loaf pan. Bake in a preheated 325 degree oven for 60 to 70 minutes. Remove from pan. Cool on a wire rack. *Yield: 1 loaf*

★ *Use unthawed frozen blueberries if fresh blueberries are unavailable.*

# Jack O'Lantern Muffins

*A different and delicious muffin*

2 1/2 cups flour
1 tablespoon pumpkin pie spice
1 teaspoon baking soda
1/2 teaspoon salt
2 eggs, beaten
1 cup pumpkin purée
1/2 cup vegetable oil
2 cups peeled and finely chopped green apples
vegetable cooking spray

Combine flour, pumpkin pie spice, baking soda and salt in a mixing bowl. Combine eggs, pumpkin purée and vegetable oil in a separate mixing bowl. Add liquid ingredients to dry ingredients. Stir until moistened. Add apples. Spoon batter into greased muffin cups filling 3/4 full. Bake in a preheated 350 degree oven for 25 to 30 minutes. *Yield: 12 muffins*

# Where There's Smoke There's Fire Corn Bread

1 ear of corn or 3/4 cup frozen corn
1 small onion, chopped
1/8 teaspoon salt
1/8 teaspoon cayenne
9 tablespoons unsalted butter, divided
1 1/4 cups milk
1 1/2 cups unbleached flour
1 cup fine cornmeal
1 tablespoon baking powder
2 1/2 tablespoons sugar
2 eggs, beaten
1/4 cup shredded smoked Cheddar cheese
1 to 2 jalapeño peppers

Sauté corn, onion, salt and cayenne in 1 tablespoon of the butter in a skillet for 5 minutes or until tender. Heat milk and the remaining butter in a saucepan until butter melts. Remove from the heat. Let mixture cool.

Combine flour, cornmeal, baking powder and sugar in a separate mixing bowl; set aside. Whisk eggs into cooled milk and butter mixture. Seed and chop jalapeño peppers. Stir into egg mixture. Add egg mixture, sautéed corn mixture and cheese to dry ingredients and mix until just blended. Batter should be lumpy.

Pour batter into a greased 9-inch round pan or cast iron skillet. Bake in a preheated 375 degree oven for 20 to 25 minutes. *Yield: 1 loaf*

★ *For extra punch, garnish with sliced jalapeño peppers.*

# Herb Cheese Muffins

1 1/2 cups flour
2 teaspoons baking powder
1/2 teaspoon salt
1/4 teaspoon pepper
2/3 cup milk
4 ounces soft spreadable herbed cream cheese
1 egg, beaten
2 teaspoons minced fresh chives

Combine flour, baking powder, salt and pepper in a mixing bowl. Combine milk, herbed cream cheese, egg and chives in a separate mixing bowl until smooth. Add the dry ingredients, stirring until just moistened. Spoon mixture into 12 muffin cups greased and floured or lined with paper muffin cups.

Bake in a preheated 375 degree oven for 15 to 20 minutes or until toothpick inserted into centers comes out clean. Remove from oven. Let stand for 10 minutes. Serve warm. *Yield: 10 to 12 muffins*

★ *Muffins also make a great appetizer. Bake batter in mini-muffin cups for 8 to 10 minutes and serve with your favorite wine.*

# Salads and Soups
★

# Salads and Soups

★

*Roasted Quail Salad with Peaches.*

# Roasted Quail Salad with Peaches

*Contributed by Nora Pouillon, Restaurant Nora*

  4  small quail
     salt and pepper
  2  tablespoons canola oil
  1  shallot, chopped
  2  fresh peaches, pitted and sliced
  1  tablespoon fresh lemon juice
  1  teaspoon chopped fresh thyme
 1/4 cup Cognac
 1/4 cup chicken broth
  8  ounces field greens
  1  cup cooked wild rice
 1/3 cup toasted pecans

Cut each quail in half, lengthwise. Season with salt and pepper. Sauté over medium heat in canola oil in a skillet for 4 to 6 minutes or until golden brown. Remove quail from skillet and keep warm. Reduce heat and sauté chopped shallot, peaches, lemon juice and thyme in skillet for 1 minute. Add Cognac and flame. Add chicken broth and remove from heat. Season with salt and pepper.

Arrange field greens on 4 plates. Make a small mound of wild rice in the center of each plate. Lean 2 halves of quail against rice mound. Spoon peach and Cognac mixture on greens and quail. Sprinkle with toasted pecans. *Yield: 4 servings*

★ *To make toasted pecans, melt 1 tablespoon butter in a skillet, add pecans and cook, stirring constantly, for 2 minutes.*

# Citrus Asparagus Salad with Spring Violets

*Springtime favorite*

  1  pound asparagus
     salt
     zest of 1 navel orange
  2  tablespoons frozen orange juice concentrate, thawed
  1  tablespoon white wine vinegar
     coarse salt
 1/4 cup olive oil
     bouquet of spring violets with stems

Cook asparagus in boiling salted water in a saucepan until crisp and tender. Immediately drain and rinse with cold water. When cool, drain and dry on a cloth towel. Place on serving platter and set aside.

Whisk orange zest, orange juice concentrate, vinegar and pinch of coarse salt in a small bowl. Slowly add olive oil, whisking to emulsify.

Pour dressing over asparagus. Place 1/2 of the bouquet of violets on platter next to asparagus. Remove stems from remaining violets and sprinkle on top of asparagus. Serve. *Yield: 4 to 6 servings*

★ *Violets can be found at specialty stores.*

# Black Bean, Squash and Corn Salad

*Crisp and colorful*

1 can (15 ounces) black beans
1 can (15 ounces) corn or 1 pound
   frozen corn
1 pound zucchini, julienne-cut
1 cup chopped red onion
1 red pepper, julienne-cut
1/4 cup white wine vinegar
1 tablespoon fresh lemon juice
1/2 cup olive oil
1 clove garlic, mashed

Rinse and drain beans. Rinse canned corn or defrost frozen corn. Combine black beans, corn, zucchini, red onion and red pepper in a serving bowl.

Whisk vinegar and lemon juice in a mixing bowl. Gradually whisk in olive oil. Add garlic. Pour dressing over salad and toss well. Cover and refrigerate several hours or up to 1 day. *Yield: 12 servings*

★ *When short on time, use Vidalia onion salad dressing and purchase the julienne-cut zucchini at a salad bar. Hearts of palm also can be substituted for zucchini.*

# New Potato and Green Bean Salad

*Easy to prepare ahead*

1 1/2 pounds small red skinned potatoes
   salt
3/4 pound haricots verts or green beans
1/4 cup balsamic vinegar
2 tablespoons Dijon mustard
2 tablespoons fresh lemon juice
1 clove garlic, minced
1/8 teaspoon Worcestershire sauce
1/2 cup olive oil
   salt and pepper
1 small red onion, coarsely chopped
1/4 cup chopped fresh basil

Steam potatoes until tender. Cool and quarter. Cook green beans in a pot of boiling salted water for 5 minutes or until crisp-tender. Transfer to a bowl of ice water and cool. Drain and cut beans in half.

Whisk vinegar, Dijon mustard, lemon juice, garlic and Worcestershire sauce in a mixing bowl. Gradually whisk in oil. Season with salt and pepper. Cover and store in refrigerator until ready to serve. Bring to room temperature before adding to the salad.

Combine potatoes, green beans, onion and fresh basil in a large bowl. Add dressing and toss to coat. Season with salt and pepper. Serve at room temperature. *Yield: 6 to 8 servings*

# Tomatoes with Basil Cream

*For the epicurean palate*

1  clove garlic
8  ounces cream cheese, softened
2  tablespoons white wine vinegar
3  tablespoons chopped fresh basil leaves
1  tablespoon chopped fresh parsley
3/4  teaspoon salt
1  teaspoon white pepper
2  red tomatoes, sliced
2  yellow tomatoes, sliced
   fresh parsley to garnish

Process garlic in a food processor or blender until finely chopped. Add cream cheese, vinegar, basil, parsley, salt and white pepper. Blend well.

Arrange tomatoes on a serving platter. Spoon dressing over tomatoes. Sprinkle with fresh parsley. Serve immediately. *Yield: 8 servings*

★  *If yellow tomatoes are unavailable, use 4 red tomatoes.*

# Roasted Corn and Wild Mushroom Salad

*Contributed by Mark Miller, Red Sage Restaurant*

2  cups medium diced Portobello mushrooms
1  tablespoon olive oil
3/4  cup sherry wine vinegar
4  cups corn
1/2  cup reconstituted sun-dried tomatoes
1  cup diced poblano chilies
1 1/2  teaspoons minced roasted garlic
1 1/2  teaspoons chipotles en adobo
1 1/2  teaspoons salt
1  teaspoon chopped fresh cilantro
1 1/2  teaspoons chopped fresh marjoram

Sauté mushrooms in olive oil over medium heat in a sauté pan. Add sherry wine vinegar to deglaze mushrooms. Set aside to cool.

Roast corn in a heavy bottomed pan. Set aside to cool.

Mix together mushrooms, corn, sun-dried tomatoes, chilies, garlic, chipotles, salt, cilantro and marjoram and serve. *Yield: 6 servings*

★  *Chipotles en adobo can be found in ethnic and gourmet grocery stores.*

# Chickpea Salad

*A symphony of spices*

3 tablespoons olive oil
¹/₄ teaspoon cumin seeds
1 medium onion, chopped
¹/₄ teaspoon ground cinnamon
¹/₄ teaspoon ground nutmeg
¹/₄ teaspoon ground cloves
1 teaspoon ground coriander
2 cloves garlic, minced
1 teaspoon grated fresh ginger
1 tablespoon tomato paste
1 can (16 ounces) chickpeas, drained
2 tablespoons water
¹/₂ teaspoon salt
¹/₈ to ¹/₄ teaspoon cayenne
1 tablespoon fresh lemon juice

Heat oil and cumin seeds over medium heat in a skillet and stir. As soon as cumin seeds start to darken, add chopped onion and cook for 7 to 8 minutes or until golden brown. Reduce heat and add cinnamon, nutmeg, cloves and coriander. Stir well. Add garlic and ginger. Cook for an additional 2 to 3 minutes. Add tomato paste, chickpeas, water, salt, cayenne and lemon juice. Cook, stirring occasionally, for an additional 10 minutes. Cool and serve at room temperature. May be prepared ahead and refrigerated. *Yield: 6 servings*

★ *Garnish with quartered tomatoes, cucumber slices, green chilies and/or onions. Chickpeas are also known as garbanzo beans.*

# Caesar Potato Salad

*A new picnic classic*

5 pounds small potatoes
  salt
1¹/₂ cups olive oil
 ¹/₄ cup fresh lemon juice
10 anchovy fillets, chopped
 2 tablespoons chopped parsley
 2 cloves garlic, crushed
 2 tablespoons Worcestershire sauce
  salt and pepper
 ³/₄ cup freshly grated Parmesan cheese
 ³/₄ cup chopped celery

Boil potatoes in lightly salted water in an 8-quart pot for 14 minutes or until tender. Drain potatoes, quarter and place in a large serving bowl.

Purée olive oil, lemon juice, anchovies, parsley, garlic and Worcestershire sauce in a blender. Season with salt and pepper. Pour over potatoes. Add Parmesan cheese and celery. Toss well. Serve warm or at room temperature. *Yield: 8 servings*

# Orzo, Shrimp, Feta and Tomato Salad

*A taste of the Mediterranean*

1  cup orzo
8  tablespoons olive oil, divided
1  pound medium shrimp, shelled and
   deveined
1/4  cup fresh lemon juice
2  tablespoons white wine vinegar
1/4  teaspoon grated fresh lemon zest
1  tablespoon chopped fresh oregano leaves
   salt and pepper
6  ounces Feta cheese, crumbled
3  tomatoes, seeded and chopped
1  cucumber, seeded and chopped
1  cup pitted sliced Kalamata olives

Prepare orzo according to package directions. Rinse, drain and chill orzo. Sauté shrimp in 2 tablespoons of the olive oil in a skillet for 2 minutes or until pink. Transfer to a bowl and refrigerate. Whisk lemon juice, vinegar, lemon zest and oregano in a mixing bowl. Season with salt and pepper. Whisk in remaining 6 tablespoons olive oil. Toss cooked orzo with dressing. Add Feta cheese, tomatoes, cucumber, olives and shrimp. Toss until combined and refrigerate up to 1 day. Serve chilled. *Yield: 4 to 6 servings*

★  *If fresh oregano is unavailable, use 1 teaspoon dried oregano.*

# Confetti Corn and Bulgur Wheat Salad

*An Eastern European surprise*

1  cup bulgur wheat
1  cup boiling water
1  clove garlic
1/4  cup olive oil
1  red apple, chopped
2  tablespoons fresh lemon juice
1/2  cup golden raisins
1  can (15 ounces) corn, drained
4  plum tomatoes, chopped
4  green onions, sliced
1/2  cup chopped fresh basil
1/4  teaspoon pepper
1/4  teaspoon salt
6  lettuce leaves

Combine bulgur wheat, water, garlic and oil in a mixing bowl. Stir and set aside for 30 minutes.

Combine apple, lemon juice and raisins in a bowl. Mix well. Fluff bulgur with fork and add to apple mixture. Add corn, tomatoes, green onions, basil, pepper and salt. Mix well. Line serving bowl with lettuce leaves. Spoon salad into serving bowl. *Yield: 8 servings*

# Chutney Melon Chicken Salad

*Only Washington could reinvent chicken salad*

1/3 cup plain yogurt
1/3 cup mango chutney
  2 cups cubed, cooked chicken
  2 cups cubed honeydew melon
  2 tablespoons shredded coconut
  6 tablespoons chopped cashews, divided
  2 tablespoons golden raisins

Combine yogurt and chutney in a bowl. Stir in chicken, melon, coconut, 4 tablespoons of the cashews and raisins. Refrigerate at least 1 hour. Just before serving, garnish with remaining 2 tablespoons cashews. Serve cold. *Yield: 4 servings*

★ *Serve in melon shells for added appeal.*

# Pecan and Wild Rice Chicken Salad

*A Southern salad*

  1 cup white and wild rice blend
2/3 cup plain yogurt
1/2 cup sliced green onions
  3 tablespoons olive oil
1/4 teaspoon grated lemon zest
11/2 tablespoons fresh lemon juice
1/2 teaspoon salt
1/4 teaspoon pepper
  2 cups shredded cooked chicken
  1 cup chopped pecans
1/2 cup dried cherries or cranberries (optional)

Prepare rice according to package directions. Set aside to cool. Combine yogurt, green onions, olive oil, lemon zest, lemon juice, salt and pepper in a serving bowl. Add cooked rice, chicken, pecans and dried cherries or cranberries. Mix well. Refrigerate until ready to serve. *Yield: 4 servings*

★ *Serve over red and green lettuce as a main course for lunch.*

# Caesar Salad with Bagel Croutons

*A fresh twist*

2 bagels
2 cloves garlic, minced
3 tablespoons butter, melted
1 1/2 tablespoons olive oil
8 cups sliced Romaine lettuce
6 tablespoons freshly grated Parmesan cheese
  Creamy Caesar Dressing (recipe at right)

Slice bagels into rounds and place on baking sheet. Sauté garlic in butter and olive oil over medium heat, stirring continuously, in a small saucepan for 2 minutes. Drizzle over bagel slices. Bake in a preheated 300 degree oven for 20 minutes or until toasted. Set aside to cool. Croutons can be prepared 1 week ahead.

Combine Romaine lettuce, Parmesan cheese and bagel croutons in a large serving bowl. Drizzle Creamy Caesar Dressing over salad and toss well. *Yield: 6 to 8 servings*

★ *Use onion or garlic bagels for a zesty kick.*

**Creamy Caesar Dressing**
1/3 cup plain yogurt
2 tablespoons fresh lemon juice
1 tablespoon balsamic vinegar
2 teaspoons Worcestershire sauce
1 teaspoon anchovy paste
1 teaspoon Dijon mustard
1/2 teaspoon freshly ground pepper
1 clove garlic, minced

Whisk ingredients in a mixing bowl. Refrigerate up to 1 week. *Yield: 1/2 cup*

★ *Dressing tastes so good, double it for next time. For an impromptu appetizer, dip sliced French bread in the dressing.*

# Raspberry Vinaigrette Salad

*Fit for a President*

¹/₂ cup sliced almonds
¹/₄ cup sugar
¹/₂ head green leaf lettuce
¹/₂ head red leaf lettuce
¹/₂ cup diced celery
1 cup halved seedless grapes
2 green onions, chopped
1 can (11 ounces) mandarin oranges, drained
¹/₂ cup chopped cucumbers
³/₄ cup Raspberry Vinaigrette (recipe at right)

Cook almonds and sugar over medium heat in a skillet until sugar caramelizes. Transfer to wax paper and cool. Crumble and set aside.

Combine lettuces, celery, grapes, green onions, mandarin oranges, cucumbers and candied almonds in a salad bowl. Toss with Raspberry Vinaigrette prior to serving. *Yield: 6 to 8 servings*

★ *Experiment with assorted lettuces, such as Romaine, radicchio, Boston, bibb or spinach.*

Raspberry Vinaigrette
2 cups seedless raspberry preserves
¹/₃ cup honey
1 cup red wine or raspberry vinegar
¹/₂ cup fresh lemon juice
1¹/₂ cups vegetable oil
1 teaspoon salt

Blend ingredients in a blender for 30 seconds or until well combined. Refrigerate up to 1 month. *Yield: 4 cups*

★ *Use extra dressing over fruit or spinach salad.*

# Bayou Salad

*A taste of Creole*

18 large shrimp
1 medium onion, finely chopped
4 tablespoons olive oil, divided
1/2 teaspoon crushed hot red pepper flakes
1 teaspoon thyme
2 bay leaves
2 cups chicken broth
1 teaspoon salt
1 cup long grain white rice
3 celery ribs, diagonally cut into
   1/2-inch pieces
1 green pepper, diced
1 red pepper, diced
4 green onions, thinly sliced
1 1/2 cups diced cooked chicken
1 1/2 cups diced cooked ham
1 large head iceberg lettuce, coarsely shredded
2 ripe tomatoes, cut into 6 wedges each
   Bayou Dressing (recipe at right)

Peel and devein shrimp, leaving tails intact. Steam for 5 minutes or until shrimp turn pink. Refrigerate until ready to serve.

Cook chopped onion in 3 tablespoons of the olive oil over medium heat in a saucepan for 5 minutes or until translucent. Add hot pepper flakes, thyme and bay leaves. Cook, stirring occasionally, for 2 to 3 minutes. Add chicken broth, salt and rice. Boil and reduce heat to low. Cover and simmer undisturbed for 20 minutes or until rice is tender and liquid is absorbed. Remove from heat and let stand covered for 5 minutes. Remove bay leaves and

transfer rice to a large serving bowl to cool. Stir occasionally. Add celery, green and red peppers, green onions, chicken, ham and the remaining tablespoon of olive oil to rice, combining well. Refrigerate up to 1 day. Serve at room temperature.

Line 6 large plates with shredded lettuce; mound 1 1/2 cups rice on top. Garnish each plate with 2 tomato wedges and 3 shrimp. Drizzle with Bayou Dressing. Serve with additional fresh pepper. Pass remaining Bayou Dressing. *Yield: 6 servings*

Bayou Dressing
1 egg
2 egg yolks
1/3 cup sherry wine vinegar
3 tablespoons whole-grain mustard
1/2 teaspoon salt
2 teaspoons freshly ground pepper
2 cups olive oil

Process egg, egg yolks, vinegar, mustard, salt and pepper in a food processor for 1 minute. Add olive oil in a steady stream while processor is running. Refrigerate until ready to serve. Dressing can be refrigerated for 3 days. Great served over seafood. *Yield: 2 1/2 cups*

# Mandarin Spinach Salad with Almonds

*Salad "Nouveau"*

3/4 cup sliced almonds
3/4 cup sugar, divided
1/2 cup red wine vinegar with herbs
2 tablespoons fresh lemon juice
1 tablespoon minced flat leaf parsley
1 cup olive oil
1 large bunch fresh spinach
2 cans (11 ounces) mandarin oranges, drained
5 green onions, chopped
1 avocado, cubed (optional)
3 slices red onion, separated into rings

Heat almonds over medium heat in a dry skillet until warm. Add 1/2 cup of the sugar. Cook 4 to 5 minutes or until sugar caramelizes and clings to almonds. Remove from heat and pour onto waxed paper. Once cooled, break into small pieces and set aside. Almonds can be prepared 3 days ahead and stored in a tightly covered container.

Whisk vinegar, lemon juice, remaining 1/4 cup sugar and parsley in a mixing bowl until smooth. Slowly add olive oil while whisking until emulsified. Do not prepare in a blender because the parsley will be too small. Dressing can be prepared 2 weeks ahead and refrigerated.

Rinse and dry spinach, remove stems and gently tear into a large salad bowl. Add mandarin oranges, green onions and avocado. Before serving, add toasted almonds and toss in dressing a little bit at a time. Add red onion rings and serve immediately.
*Yield: 6 to 8 servings*

★ *Double the almond recipe and serve alone, on top of ice cream or sprinkled into oatmeal.*

# Wilted Lettuce

*An old family treasure*

8 cups torn red and green leaf lettuce
8 green onions, chopped
8 slices bacon
1/2 cup white vinegar
2 tablespoons plus 2 teaspoons brown sugar
6 cherry tomatoes, halved

Combine lettuce and green onions in a serving bowl. Set aside. Cook bacon over medium heat in a skillet until crisp. Remove bacon, reserving drippings in skillet. Crumble bacon and sprinkle over lettuce.

Add vinegar and brown sugar to bacon drippings in skillet. Boil, stirring constantly, until sugar dissolves. Pour dressing over lettuce and toss gently. Garnish with cherry tomatoes. Serve immediately.
*Yield: 8 servings*

# Oyster Bisque

*A gift from the Chesapeake*

1/2 cup uncooked long grain rice
4 cups chicken broth
4 tablespoons butter
18 oysters, shucked, reserve liquid
   salt and pepper
3 dashes Tabasco
1 1/2 cups heavy cream
1/4 cup Cognac
1 tablespoon chopped fresh parsley

Cook rice in chicken broth in a saucepan until done. Add butter. Drain rice and discard broth. Finely chop 12 oysters. Add to cooked rice. Season with salt and pepper. Add Tabasco. Add heavy cream. Heat over medium heat just to the point of boiling. Add remaining oysters. Heat until oysters curl at the edges. Add Cognac and simmer for 2 minutes. Ladle soup into heated soup bowls, making sure 1 whole oyster is in each bowl. Garnish with parsley.
*Yield: 6 servings*

★ *In lieu of shucking fresh oysters, a pint of oysters with liquid may be used.*

# Rosemary Butternut Squash Soup

*Warm autumn colors in your kitchen*

2 large butternut squash
1 tablespoon vegetable oil
6 cups chicken broth
1 tablespoon finely chopped fresh rosemary
2 teaspoons grated orange zest
   salt and pepper
2 tablespoons sour cream
2 tablespoons heavy cream
   fresh rosemary sprigs to garnish

Cut butternut squash in half. Peel, seed and scoop out fibers. Coat inside with vegetable oil. Place, cut-side down, on a baking sheet. Roast in a preheated 375 degree for 25 minutes or until tender. Transfer to an 8-quart pot. Add chicken broth, rosemary and orange zest. Boil over medium-high heat. Reduce heat and simmer for 30 minutes. Transfer to a food processor or blender and process until smooth. Season with salt and pepper. Return to pot to keep warm or ladle soup into bowls. Combine sour cream and heavy cream in a mixing bowl. Decoratively swirl a small amount of cream mixture into soup to garnish. Garnish with fresh rosemary sprigs. Serve hot. *Yield: 4 servings*

*Rosemary Butternut Squash Soup.*

# Potato Garlic Soup with Rosemary Butter

*Elegant soup for a winter evening*

  3 cups chicken broth
  1 pound russet potatoes, peeled and diced
20 garlic cloves, peeled
1/2 cup milk
1/2 cup heavy cream
    salt and pepper
  2 tablespoons unsalted butter, softened
1 1/2 teaspoons chopped fresh rosemary

Boil chicken broth, potatoes and garlic in an 8-quart pot. Reduce heat and simmer for 15 minutes or until tender. Remove from heat. Purée in a blender or food processor until smooth and creamy. Return to pot. Add milk and heavy cream and heat thoroughly. Do not boil. Season with salt and pepper.

Mix butter and chopped rosemary together in a mixing bowl. Serve soup topped with a teaspoon of rosemary butter. *Yield: 4 servings*

# Artichoke and Mushroom Soup

*A sophisticated soup*

  1 can (15 ounces) artichoke hearts
  1 pound fresh mushrooms, sliced thin
1/4 cup sliced green onions
1/2 cup butter
  2 tablespoons chopped fresh parsley
  3 tablespoons flour
  3 cups chicken broth
  1 cup half and half
    salt and pepper
  1 tablespoon hot sauce

Drain, rinse and quarter artichoke hearts. Sauté artichoke hearts, mushrooms and green onions in butter over medium heat in an 8-quart pot for 5 to 10 minutes or until green onions are translucent. Add parsley and flour, stirring well. Purée mixture in a blender or food processor and return to pot. Slowly add chicken broth and half and half. Bring to a boil. Immediately reduce heat and simmer until thoroughly heated, stirring occasionally. Season with salt and pepper. Stir in hot sauce. Serve hot. *Yield: 6 to 8 servings*

★ *If prepared a day ahead, slowly reheat until hot.*

# Italian Soup

*A visit to Tuscany*

1¹/2 pounds sweet or hot bulk Italian sausage
  1 cup chopped onion
  2 cloves garlic, minced
  4 ripe tomatoes, chopped
  1 can (14 ounces) tomato sauce
  7 cups beef broth
  1 cup sliced carrots
  1 cup sliced celery
  1 teaspoon dried basil
  1 teaspoon dried oregano
  2 cups sliced zucchini
  1 cup sliced fresh mushrooms
  1 green pepper, diced
¹/4 cup chopped fresh parsley
  2 cups frozen tortellini or small ravioli

Brown sausage, onion and garlic in an 8-quart pot. Drain fat from pot and return to stove. Add tomatoes, tomato sauce, beef broth, carrots, celery, basil and oregano. Simmer for 30 minutes. Add zucchini, mushrooms, green pepper and parsley. Simmer for an additional 50 minutes. Just before serving, add frozen tortellini or small ravioli. Simmer for 10 minutes or until pasta is cooked.
*Yield: 12 servings*

# Mexican Corn Chowder

*A spicy soup*

  3 cans (14¹/2 ounces) creamed corn
  1 can (14 ounces) stewed tomatoes
  1 can (14 ounces) chicken broth
  2 cans (4 ounces) chopped green chilies
1¹/2 teaspoons garlic powder
  2 cups cubed cooked chicken or turkey
  1 teaspoon pepper
1¹/2 teaspoons dried oregano
  2 cups half and half
  4 cups shredded Monterey Jack cheese

Combine and cook creamed corn, tomatoes, chicken broth, green chilies, garlic powder, chicken, pepper and oregano over medium heat in an 8-quart pot. When hot, reduce heat to low. Add half and half. Stir. Add cheese and stir until melted. Serve hot.
*Yield: 8 servings*

★ *Add 1 to 2 peeled and seeded jalapeño peppers to the soup for extra zip.*

# Black Bean Soup

*Healthy and hearty*

2 tablespoons olive oil
2 cloves garlic, minced
1 large onion, chopped
1 red or green pepper, chopped
1 can (14¹/₂ ounces) chopped tomatoes
1 tablespoon dried thyme
4 cans (16 ounces) black beans, drained and rinsed
2 to 3 cups chicken broth, divided
  salt and pepper
2 green onions, sliced

Heat olive oil, garlic, onion and red or green pepper over medium heat in an 8-quart pot. Sauté for 10 minutes or until onion is tender. Add tomatoes with their juices and thyme. Reduce heat. Simmer for 10 minutes or until vegetables are very soft. Add black beans and 2 cups of the chicken broth. Purée mixture, in a blender or food processor, in batches, until smooth. Return to pot and simmer. Thin soup with the remaining 1 cup chicken broth if necessary. Season with salt and pepper. Garnish with a sprinkle of green onions. Serve hot. *Yield: 4 servings*

# Mulligatawny Soup

*Curry powder adds kick*

¹/₄ cup finely chopped onion
1 tablespoon curry powder
2 tablespoons vegetable oil
1 tart apple, peeled, cored and chopped
¹/₄ cup chopped carrots
2 tablespoons chopped green pepper
3 tablespoons flour
4 cups chicken broth
1 can (16 ounces) tomatoes, chopped and undrained
1 tablespoon chopped fresh parsley
2 teaspoons lemon juice
1 teaspoon sugar
2 whole cloves
  salt and pepper
1 cup diced cooked chicken or turkey

Cook onion and curry powder in vegetable oil in an 8-quart pot until onion is tender. Add apple, carrots and green pepper. Cook, stirring occasionally, for 5 minutes or until vegetables are crisp-tender. Add flour and mix well. Add chicken broth, tomatoes, parsley, lemon juice, sugar and cloves. Season with salt and pepper. Boil. Add cooked chicken, reduce heat and simmer for 30 minutes. *Yield: 6 servings*

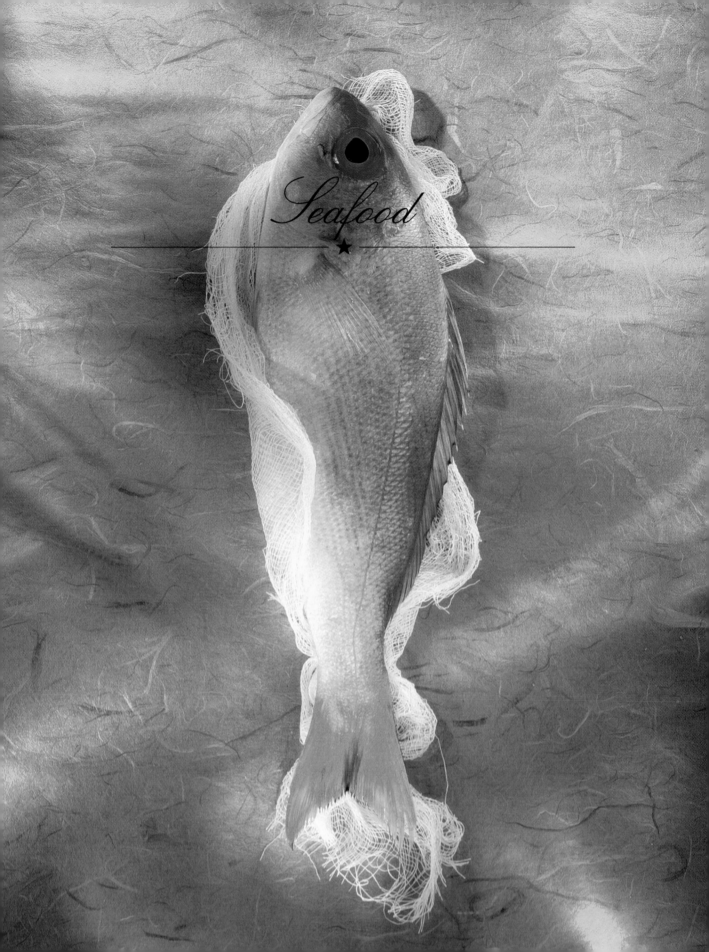

Seafood

# Seafood

★

Kinkead's Crab Cakes.

# Kinkead's Crab Cakes

*Contributed by Robert Kinkead, Kinkead's*

1 small red pepper, finely chopped
1/4 cup finely chopped onion
1 large shallot, minced
1 clove garlic, minced
3 tablespoons peanut oil
3 pounds jumbo lump crab meat, cleaned
1 egg, beaten
1/8 teaspoon cayenne
4 dashes Tabasco
   salt and pepper
3 cups bread crumbs
4 tablespoons butter
   Mustard Sauce (recipe at right)
   Corn and Cherry Tomato Relish
   (recipe at right)

Sauté red pepper, onion, shallot and garlic in peanut oil over high heat in a skillet. Set aside to cool. Gently combine red pepper mixture, crab meat, egg, cayenne and Tabasco in a mixing bowl. Season with salt and pepper. Form into 6 crab cake patties. Dredge crab cakes in bread crumbs. Refrigerate for 1 hour. Sauté crab cakes in butter in a large skillet until golden on each side. Serve with Mustard Sauce and Corn and Cherry Tomato Relish on the side. *Yield: 6 crab cakes*

★ *Can also be used as an appetizer by forming crab mixture into 12 small crab cakes.*

Mustard Sauce
3/4 cup mayonnaise
1 tablespoon red wine vinegar
1/2 teaspoon Old Bay Seasoning
1/2 teaspoon chili powder
2 tablespoons Dijon mustard
2 tablespoons honey
1 tablespoon chopped fresh parsley
   pepper

Combine first 7 ingredients in a mixing bowl. Season with pepper. Set aside. *Yield: 1 cup*

Corn and Cherry Tomato Relish
24 cherry tomatoes, halved
4 ears corn, shucked and blanched
3 green onions, chopped
1 small onion, finely diced
1 tablespoon chopped fresh parsley
1 teaspoon sugar
1/4 cup red wine vinegar
   salt and pepper

Combine first 7 ingredients in a mixing bowl. Season with salt and pepper and set aside. *Yield: 2 cups*

# Shrimp Diane

*Simple yet sophisticated*

1 pound medium shrimp with shells
2 cups water
3/4 cup unsalted butter, divided
1/4 cup chopped green onions
3/4 teaspoon salt
1/2 teaspoon minced garlic
1/2 teaspoon cayenne
1/4 teaspoon white pepper
1/4 teaspoon black pepper
1/4 teaspoon dried basil
1/4 teaspoon dried thyme
1/8 teaspoon dried oregano
1/2 pound fresh mushrooms, sliced
3 tablespoons chopped fresh parsley

Peel shrimp and reserve shells. Refrigerate shrimp until needed. Boil shells in 2 cups of water for 20 minutes in a saucepan. Strain and cool liquid. Reserve to make shrimp stock.

Melt 1/2 cup of the butter over high heat in a skillet. Add green onions, salt, garlic, ground peppers, basil, thyme and oregano, stirring well. Add shrimp. Shake skillet in a back and forth motion for 1 minute or until shrimp turn pink. Add mushrooms and 4 tablespoons of the shrimp stock. Add the remaining 1/4 cup butter in chunks and continue shaking skillet. Before butter completely melts, add parsley and 2 tablespoons of the shrimp stock. Continue shaking skillet until ingredients are mixed thoroughly and the sauce is the consistency of cream. Serve immediately in a bowl with sliced French bread on the side or over pasta or rice. *Yield: 4 servings*

★ *Shrimp stock also can be purchased at gourmet grocery stores.*

# Swordfish with Parmesan Crust

*Simply delicious*

1 cup plus 2 tablespoons flour, divided
1/4 teaspoon salt
1/8 teaspoon pepper
2 1/2 cups freshly shredded Parmesan cheese
3 eggs
1/4 cup milk
1/2 cup butter
4 (7 ounces each) swordfish steaks
lemon wedges for garnish

Combine 1 cup of the flour with salt and pepper in a mixing bowl. Combine Parmesan cheese with the remaining 2 tablespoons flour in a separate mixing bowl. Whisk eggs and milk together in third mixing bowl. Dredge swordfish steaks in flour, shaking off excess. Dip floured swordfish steaks in egg mixture. Then dredge in Parmesan cheese mixture. Place steaks on a baking sheet lined with wax paper until ready to cook.

Sauté swordfish steaks in butter over medium-high heat in a large nonstick skillet for 2 minutes on each side or until golden. Transfer partially cooked swordfish steaks to a clean baking sheet.

Bake in a preheated 350 degree oven for approximately 6 to 9 minutes or until cooked through. Garnish with lemon wedges.
*Yield: 4 servings*

★ *Perfect served with rice pilaf or orzo.*

# Shrimp in Cajun Red Gravy

*A delicious alternative to shrimp Creole*

 1 pound large shrimp, shelled and deveined
 5 teaspoons Cajun seafood seasoning, divided
 2 tablespoons unsalted butter
 1 cup finely chopped onion
 1/2 cup chopped green pepper
 1/4 cup chopped celery
 2 bay leaves
 1 tablespoon minced garlic
 2 cups canned crushed tomatoes
 1 tablespoon dark brown sugar
 1 1/2 cups shrimp stock

Combine shrimp and 2 teaspoons of the Cajun seafood seasoning in a mixing bowl. Set aside.

Melt butter over high heat in a skillet until sizzling. Add onion, green pepper, celery, 3 teaspoons of the Cajun seafood seasoning and bay leaves. Cook, stirring occasionally, for 6 minutes. Add garlic and crushed tomatoes. Cook for an additional 8 minutes. Add brown sugar and shrimp stock. Boil sauce. Add shrimp and cook for 2 minutes or until shrimp turn pink. Cover and turn off heat. Let stand for 5 minutes while shrimp finishes cooking and flavors blend. Serve immediately over rice or pasta. *Yield: 4 servings*

★ *Shrimp stock can be purchased at gourmet grocery stores or made by boiling discarded shrimp shells in 3 cups water for 20 minutes and straining.*

# Scallops with Garlic and Sun-Dried Tomatoes

*Quick and elegant*

 1 1/2 pounds scallops
    salt and pepper
 1 cup oil-packed, sun-dried tomatoes
 1/4 cup olive oil
 2 tablespoons chopped garlic
 1 whole lemon, juiced
 2 1/2 tablespoons butter
 3 tablespoons chopped fresh parsley

Rinse and drain scallops. Season with salt and pepper. Drain and chop sun-dried tomatoes. Just before serving, heat a large skillet until very hot. Add scallops and olive oil. Immediately add garlic. Do not stir. Cook for 40 seconds. Add sun-dried tomatoes. Stir for 30 seconds. Add lemon juice, butter and parsley. Remove skillet from stove. Stir until butter melts. Serve immediately. *Yield: 4 servings*

★ *Prepare ingredients before starting, to avoid overcooking scallops.*

# Black Pearl Salmon and Sea Scallops

*Contributed by Neal Corman, Blue Point Grille and Sutton Place Gourmet*

5 cups diced leeks
1/2 cup red wine vinegar
1 cup red wine
1 fresh herb sachet (see note)
6 tablespoons butter
   salt and pepper
6 extra large sea scallops
4 tablespoons olive oil, divided
1/2 cup fresh lemon juice, divided
8 ounces crème fraîche
1/4 cup fresh dill, chopped
4 (6 ounces each) black pearl salmon fillets
2 ounces salmon roe

Boil leeks, vinegar, red wine, herb sachet, butter and pinch of salt in a saucepan. Reduce heat. Simmer until leeks are soft and liquid almost evaporates. Set aside.

Slice each scallop into 3 layers. Marinate in a sauté pan with 2 tablespoons of the olive oil, lemon juice and pinch of pepper for 15 minutes.

Heat crème fraîche in a saucepan until liquefied. Add dill and a dash of lemon juice. Season with salt and pepper. Remove from the heat and keep warm.

Sprinkle salmon fillets with salt and pepper. Sauté in the remaining 2 tablespoons olive oil in a skillet until lightly colored on both sides. Place fillets in an ovenproof baking dish. Bake in a preheated 350 degree oven until cooked to medium-rare. Heat scallops in their sauté pan for 2 minutes or until scallops turn white.

While salmon and scallops are cooking, remove herb sachet from leeks and reheat. Season with salt and pepper.

When salmon is cooked, remove from oven and place on a serving plate. Top each fillet with a 1/3-inch layer of leeks. Arrange scallops on leeks. Pour sauce around the plate. Garnish with a dollop of salmon roe. *Yield: 4 servings*

★ *Tie fresh parsley, thyme, black peppercorns and a bay leaf in a square of cheesecloth to create a fresh herb sachet.*

## Aegean Shrimp

*For shrimp and Feta lovers*

- 2 cups chopped onion
- 1/2 cup chopped celery
- 2 cloves garlic, minced
- 1/4 cup olive oil
- 1 red or green pepper, julienne-cut
- 1 can (28 ounces) plum tomatoes, chopped
- 1/2 cup finely chopped fresh parsley
- 1 can (8 ounces) tomato sauce
- 1 teaspoon dried oregano
  salt and pepper
- 1/2 cup dry white wine
- 2 pounds large shrimp, cleaned and cooked
- 2 cups crumbled Feta cheese

Sauté onion, celery and garlic in olive oil over medium heat in a skillet. Add red pepper and sauté until soft. Add plum tomatoes, parsley, tomato sauce and oregano. Season with salt and pepper. Simmer sauce for 20 minutes or until thick. Add white wine and simmer 5 additional minutes.

Pour 1 inch of sauce into a 9x13-inch greased ovenproof baking dish. Layer shrimp in dish. Pour remaining sauce over shrimp. Sprinkle with Feta cheese. Bake in a preheated 400 degree oven for 15 to 20 minutes. Then broil for 2 minutes or until golden. Serve over pasta, rice or orzo.
*Yield: 8 servings*

## Thai Shrimp and Spinach Curry

*Tantalizingly tasty*

- 1 can (14 ounces) unsweetened coconut milk, chilled
- 2 teaspoons Thai red curry paste
- 1 pound large shrimp, shelled and deveined
- 2 tablespoons nam pla fish sauce
- 2 carrots, thinly sliced
- 1 red pepper, thinly sliced
- 3/4 pound fresh spinach, cleaned and spun dry
- 3 tablespoons chopped cilantro

Spoon 1/3 cup of the thick coconut cream from top of chilled coconut milk into a skillet. Cook over medium heat, whisking constantly, for 2 to 3 minutes. Add curry paste, whisking for 1 minute. Add shrimp. Sauté over medium-high heat for 2 minutes or until the shrimp turn light pink. Add the remaining coconut milk and nam pla fish sauce. Simmer, uncovered and stirring occasionally, for 1 minute or until shrimp is thoroughly cooked. Transfer shrimp with slotted spoon to a serving bowl. Tent bowl with aluminum foil to keep warm.

Add sliced carrots and red pepper to same skillet. Simmer for 5 minutes. Add fresh spinach in batches, stirring until each batch is wilted. Return cooked shrimp to skillet and simmer, stirring occasionally, for 1 minute. Sprinkle with cilantro. Serve over rice.
*Yield: 4 servings*

★ *Thai red curry paste and nam pla fish sauce are available in ethnic and gourmet grocery stores.*

*Thai Shrimp and Spinach Curry.*

# Salmon en Croûte

*Beautiful company dish*

4 (8 ounces each) thick salmon fillets, skin removed
1 cup white wine
1 small sweet onion, thinly sliced
2 tablespoons butter
1 pound fresh asparagus
2 packages (17 ounces each) puff pastry sheets, thawed
Cucumber Sauce (recipe at right)

Place salmon fillets and wine in a large skillet. Cover and steam for 2 minutes. Set aside to cool. Sauté onion in butter in a skillet for 2 minutes. Set aside. Peel asparagus. If asparagus is thick, then briefly steam or blanch. Cut asparagus into approximate length of salmon fillets.

Lay out all four puff pastry sheets. Dust pastry with flour and roll with a rolling pin until each pastry sheet is approximately twice as big as a salmon fillet.

Divide asparagus among puff pastry sheets. Lay asparagus in a single layer on the right side of each pastry square. Place one cooked salmon fillet over asparagus. Top with cooked onions. Fold left side of pastry over salmon. Press edges down to eliminate air pockets. Seal with fingertips. Bake pastry packets on a lightly greased baking sheet in a preheated 400 degree oven for 18 to 20 minutes or until puffed and golden. Serve with Cucumber Sauce. *Yield: 4 servings*

Cucumber Sauce
1/2 tablespoon minced shallots
1 tablespoon butter
1/3 cup chopped, seeded peeled cucumber
2 tablespoons flour
1 pint heavy cream
1 tablespoon chopped fresh dill

Sauté shallots in butter over medium heat in a saucepan for 1 minute. Add cucumber and cook for 1 minute. Stir in flour. Cook for 3 minutes until incorporated. Add heavy cream and cook, stirring occasionally, for 8 minutes. Sauce will thicken slightly. Add dill just before serving. *Yield: 1 1/2 cups*

★ *If fresh dill is unavailable, use 1 teaspoon dried dill.*

## Salmon with Cucumbers

*Perfect for the busy chef*

2 shallots, chopped
2 tablespoons vegetable oil
1/2 teaspoon pepper
1/2 teaspoon salt
1 tablespoon lemon juice
4 (6 ounces each) salmon fillets
1 cucumber, peeled, seeded and thinly sliced
1 tablespoon chopped fresh dill
2 tablespoons red wine vinegar

Microwave shallots and oil in an 7x11-inch microwaveable baking dish on High for 2 to 3 minutes. Stir in pepper, salt and lemon juice. Coat salmon fillets with mixture. Arrange skin side down with thinner ends toward center of baking dish. Top with sliced cucumber. Cover and microwave on High for 5 to 7 minutes or until opaque. Let stand, covered, for 2 minutes. Sprinkle dill and red wine vinegar on top. *Yield: 4 servings*

★ *Also great served cold.*

## Grilled Swordfish with Spicy Salsa

*Great for summer entertaining*

4 (8 ounces each) Swordfish steaks
2 tablespoons olive oil
  salt and pepper
  Spicy Salsa (recipe follows)

Rub swordfish steaks with olive oil. Season with salt and pepper. Prepare a very hot grill. Grill swordfish steaks until opaque. Serve with Spicy Salsa.
*Yield: 4 servings*

Spicy Salsa
7 fresh tomatillos, skin removed and chopped
1 large Anaheim pepper, seeded and chopped
1 jalapeño pepper, seeded and chopped
1 medium red onion, chopped
2 cloves garlic, minced
1/4 cup chopped fresh cilantro
  salt

Mix first 6 ingredients in a mixing bowl. Season with salt. Let stand for 2 to 3 hours at room temperature.
*Yield: 2 cups*

# Grilled Salmon on Vidalia Onions

*An impressive seasonal dish*

  4 (8 ounces each) salmon fillets
1 1/4 cups Vidalia Onion Salad Dressing, divided
  3 tablespoons olive oil
  2 tablespoons butter
  8 cups sliced Vidalia onions
1/4 cup water

Marinate salmon fillets in 1/2 cup Vidalia Onion Salad Dressing for at least 15 minutes or refrigerate overnight.

Cook sliced onions in olive oil and butter over medium heat in a skillet, stirring often, until translucent. After 7 minutes, add water and continue to cook until very tender. Do not let onions brown. Remove skillet from heat. Stir in 1/3 cup Vidalia Onion Salad Dressing. Cover to keep warm.

Prepare a very hot grill. Place salmon fillets, skin side down, on grill. Discard marinade. Cook salmon undisturbed. Salmon will take approximately 10 to 12 minutes per inch to cook. Salmon fillets should flake when fully cooked. Remove salmon fillets from grill. The skin may remain on grill.

Spread 1/4 of the cooked onions on a dinner plate and top with a grilled salmon fillet. Drizzle with Vidalia Onion Salad Dressing. Repeat with each fillet. *Yield: 4 servings*

★ *Vidalia Onion Salad Dressing is available in the gourmet section of large grocery stores. Use another sweet onion such as Maui or Walla Walla if Vidalia onions are not available.*

# Grilled Lime Tuna Kabobs

*An unusual shish kabob*

1 1/4 pounds tuna steak, 1-inch thick
  2 red peppers
12 shallots or small onions, peeled
12 whole fresh mushrooms
  1 lime, juiced and zested
1/4 cup olive oil
  4 teaspoons chopped fresh rosemary
  2 cloves garlic, chopped

Rinse tuna and pat dry. Cut tuna into 1-inch cubes. Cut red peppers into 16 pieces. Place tuna cubes, shallots, mushrooms and red peppers in a mixing bowl. Combine lime juice, olive oil, rosemary and garlic in a blender or small food processor until emulsified. Pour over tuna and vegetables and combine well. Add lime zest. Marinate for 30 minutes in refrigerator.

Thread tuna and vegetables onto skewers, alternating tuna with pieces of vegetables. Pour any remaining marinade over prepared skewers. Before grilling, drain excess marinade from skewers.

Oil grill with olive oil and preheat. Grill skewers for 6 to 8 minutes, turning once. Remove from grill. Tuna should be slightly pink inside. Serve immediately with rice. *Yield: 4 servings*

★ *Leftover tuna and vegetables are great on toasted, crusty bread.*

# Poultry and Meats

★

# Poultry and Meats

★

Sesame Chicken Kabobs

## Sesame Chicken Kabobs

*Perfect for a summer cookout*

1/4 cup low-sodium soy sauce
1/3 cup olive oil
1/2 cup Vermouth
1/4 cup light corn syrup
2 1/2 tablespoons sesame seeds
1 tablespoon garlic paste
2 tablespoons lemon juice
1/4 teaspoon ground ginger
6 boneless, skinless chicken breasts, cubed
1 small pineapple, cut into 1-inch cubes
1 red pepper, cut into 1/2-inch squares
1 yellow pepper, cut into 1/2-inch squares
1/2 pound fresh mushroom caps
12 cherry tomatoes

Combine soy sauce, olive oil, Vermouth, corn syrup, sesame seeds, garlic paste, lemon juice, ginger and chicken in a resealable plastic bag. Marinate in the refrigerator overnight.

Alternate chicken with pineapple and vegetables on skewers, beginning and ending with pineapple or a vegetable.

Prepare a very hot grill. Grill kabobs, basting with remaining marinade, until chicken is cooked through. Serve with rice pilaf. *Yield: 6 to 8 servings*

## Chicken with Smoked Mozzarella

*A great way to enjoy summer's abundance*

4 boneless, skinless chicken breasts
1/3 cup flour
1/2 teaspoon salt
1/4 teaspoon pepper
1/2 cup milk
1/2 cup cornmeal
2 tablespoons olive oil
16 fresh basil leaves
8 slices tomatoes
salt and pepper
4 slices smoked Mozzarella cheese

Flatten chicken with a meat mallet until thin. Combine flour, 1/2 teaspoon salt and 1/4 teaspoon pepper in a shallow bowl. Place milk and cornmeal each in separate shallow bowls. Dredge chicken consecutively in seasoned flour, milk and cornmeal.

Brown chicken on both sides in olive oil over medium-high heat in a skillet. Place cooked chicken in an ovenproof baking dish. Top each with 4 basil leaves and 2 tomato slices. Season with salt and pepper. Top with smoked Mozzarella cheese. Broil until cheese is golden and bubbling. *Yield: 4 servings*

# Grilled Teriyaki Chicken

4 boneless, skinless chicken breasts
1/3 cup soy sauce
1/4 cup teriyaki sauce
1 tomato, chopped and seeded
3 green onions, chopped
1/2 cup shredded Cheddar cheese

Marinate chicken breasts in soy sauce and teriyaki sauce in a resealable plastic bag for 30 minutes or refrigerate overnight. Grill or broil over high heat about 5 minutes per side. Chicken should be slightly undercooked. Place chicken in an 8x8-inch ovenproof baking dish and discard marinade. Sprinkle 1/4 of the tomato, green onions and Cheddar cheese over each piece of chicken. Broil for 3 to 5 minutes, until chicken is thoroughly cooked and cheese is melted and bubbly. Serve immediately. *Yield: 4 servings*

★ *For a change of pace, use 1/4 cup soy sauce and 1/3 cup barbecue sauce to marinate chicken. After grilling, top each chicken breast with 1 tablespoon barbecue sauce, 1 tablespoon crumbled cooked bacon, green onions and Cheddar cheese. Broil and serve immediately.*

# Broiled Yogurt Chicken

*A taste of the Middle East*

1 cup plain yogurt
1/4 teaspoon minced garlic
1 green onion, chopped
1 teaspoon dried oregano
1 tablespoon olive oil
1 tablespoon white wine vinegar
1 teaspoon salt
1/8 teaspoon pepper
4 boneless, skinless chicken breasts
1/2 cup crumbled Feta cheese
   fresh oregano or parsley to garnish

Combine yogurt, garlic, green onion, oregano, olive oil, vinegar, salt, pepper and chicken in a resealable plastic bag. Marinate 15 minutes or refrigerate overnight.

Place chicken breasts in broiling pan. Broil in a preheated broiler for 4 to 5 minutes. Turn chicken breasts over and brush with remaining yogurt mixture. Sprinkle with crumbled Feta cheese. Broil an additional 5 to 6 minutes or until the chicken is tender and lightly browned. Arrange cooked chicken breasts on warm serving platter. Garnish with oregano or parsley sprigs. *Yield: 4 servings*

★ *Easily doubled.*

# Chicken with Tomatoes and White Wine

*A Mediterranean treat*

4 boneless, skinless chicken breasts
3 tablespoons butter
2 tablespoons olive oil
1 tablespoon fresh chopped rosemary
  salt and pepper
2 garlic cloves, crushed
2 tablespoons chopped shallots
1/4 cup fresh quartered mushrooms
1 (14 ounces) can Italian plum tomatoes
1/2 cup chicken broth
3/4 cup white wine

Brown chicken in butter and olive oil over medium heat in a skillet. Season with rosemary, salt and pepper. Transfer to a platter and keep warm.

Sauté garlic and shallots in the remaining oil in the same skillet. Add mushrooms and tomatoes and their juices and cook 5 minutes. Add chicken broth and white wine. Cook 10 minutes or until the sauce is reduced. Return chicken to skillet for 3 minutes to absorb the flavor. Transfer chicken to a warmed serving platter and top with sauce. *Yield: 4 servings*

# Sautéed Chicken with Buttered Pecans

*A taste of the South*

4 boneless, skinless chicken breasts
  salt and pepper
3 tablespoons butter, divided
1/2 cup minced shallots
1/2 cup chopped pecans
1 1/2 teaspoons dried rubbed sage
2/3 cup dry white wine
2/3 cup chicken broth

Season chicken with salt and pepper. Sauté chicken in 2 tablespoons of the butter in a skillet over medium-high heat about 3 to 5 minutes per side or until chicken browns and is cooked. Set aside chicken and keep warm.

Sauté shallots, pecans and sage in remaining 1 tablespoon melted butter in same skillet for 2 minutes or until pecans begin to brown. Add white wine and chicken broth. Increase heat to high and boil sauce for 8 minutes or until reduced to syrup consistency. Spoon pecan sauce over chicken. Serve immediately. *Yield: 4 servings*

# Autumn Chicken

*A seasonal favorite*

8 to 10 chicken pieces
  salt and pepper
2 tablespoons butter, melted
2 cups orange juice
1 1/2 cups sugar
1/2 cup dry Sherry
1 can (16 ounces) yams, reserve 1/2 cup syrup
1 teaspoon ground cinnamon
1 teaspoon ground nutmeg
1/4 teaspoon ground ginger
1 pound fresh cranberries, divided
1 medium fresh orange, thinly sliced with peel
1 1/2 cups fresh baby carrots, sliced
1 tablespoon cornstarch

Season chicken with salt and pepper. Brown chicken in butter over medium heat in a skillet for 10 to 15 minutes. Remove chicken and set aside. Drain fat. Boil orange juice, sugar, Sherry, the reserved yam syrup, cinnamon, nutmeg, ginger and 1 1/2 cups cranberries in same skillet. Add cooked chicken, orange slices and carrots. Lower heat and simmer for 30 minutes. Add the remaining fresh cranberries and yams and cook for 10 minutes. Remove 1/2 cup of sauce to a small mixing bowl. Add cornstarch and stir until smooth. Pour into skillet and stir 3 to 5 minutes or until sauce thickens. Serve immediately. *Yield: 6 to 8 servings*

# Champagne Chicken and Shrimp

*Champagne adds pizzazz*

2 pounds fresh shrimp, shelled and deveined
3 tablespoons lemon juice
1 1/2 tablespoons salt
2 green onions, chopped
3 whole chickens or 8 chicken breasts
4 tablespoons butter, divided
3/4 pound fresh mushrooms, sliced
1 1/2 cups water
1/3 cup flour
1 chicken bouillon cube
1 1/2 cups half and half
3/4 cup champagne
  pinch of fresh rosemary or tarragon
1/2 cup shredded Gruyère cheese

Marinate shrimp in lemon juice, salt and green onions for 30 minutes in refrigerator. Brown chicken in 2 tablespoons of the butter over medium heat in a skillet until cooked through. Transfer to an ovenproof baking dish and set aside. Cook shrimp in the same skillet for 5 minutes or until pink. Add to chicken in baking dish. Add remaining 2 tablespoons butter to same skillet and sauté sliced mushrooms. Reserve. Combine water, flour and chicken bouillon cube over medium heat in a saucepan. Gradually add half and half and champagne, stirring until smooth. Season with fresh rosemary or tarragon. Add cooked mushrooms. Pour mushroom sauce over cooked chicken and shrimp. Reheat in a 350 degree oven for 10 minutes. Top with grated Gruyère cheese and broil until melted. Serve with rice. *Yield: 8 servings*

## Capital Chicken

6  boneless, skinless chicken breasts
6  squares (1/2 ounce) Cheddar cheese
6  squares (1/2 ounce) Swiss cheese
1/4  cup flour
1/2  teaspoon salt
1/4  teaspoon pepper
1  egg, beaten
1/8  cup milk
1/2  cup fine dry bread crumbs
1/2  cup butter
   toothpicks

Flatten chicken with a meat mallet until thin. Place a square of each cheese in center of each chicken. Fold short ends of chicken over cheeses, followed by long ends. Secure with toothpicks.

Combine flour, salt and pepper in a shallow bowl. Combine egg and milk in a separate shallow bowl. Place bread crumbs in a third shallow bowl. Dredge each chicken breast consecutively in flour mixture, egg mixture and then bread crumbs. Allow chicken to stand for 15 to 30 minutes to set coating.

Sauté chicken in butter over medium heat in a skillet for 5 to 7 minutes on each side or until golden brown.

Place chicken in an ovenproof shallow baking dish. Pour remaining butter from skillet over the chicken. Do not add brown residue from bottom of skillet. Bake in a preheated 325 degree oven for 25 minutes or until tender. *Yield: 6 servings*

## Baked Chicken Marsala

*Marsala adds unique taste*

1  egg
1/4  cup milk
4  boneless, skinless chicken breasts
1/2  cup flour
1 1/2  cups Italian-style bread crumbs
4  tablespoons butter
1/2  cup Marsala wine
8  fresh mushrooms, sliced
1  small onion, sliced

Beat egg and milk in a shallow bowl. Coat chicken pieces with flour; dip in egg mixture and coat with bread crumbs. Place chicken in a greased ovenproof baking dish. Dot each piece of chicken with 1 tablespoon butter. Bake in a preheated 350 degree oven for 20 minutes or until the chicken is almost cooked through.

Pour Marsala wine over chicken. Top with sliced mushrooms and onions. Cover with aluminum foil and bake an additional 5 to 10 minutes. Serve immediately with pasta or rice. *Yield: 4 servings*

★ *This can also be prepared with chicken drumsticks or breasts and baked for 45 minutes.*

# White Bean Chicken Chili

*Contributed by Robert McGowan, Old Ebbitt Grill*

1 pound white navy beans
1 small red pepper, diced
1 small green pepper, diced
1 medium Spanish onion, diced
4 tablespoons olive oil, divided
7 cups chicken stock
2 cloves garlic, minced
3 teaspoons ground cumin, divided
3 teaspoons chili powder, divided
3 plum tomatoes, chopped
   salt and pepper to taste
3 (14 to 16 ounces) whole bone-in
   chicken breasts
1  tablespoon diced garlic
6 tablespoons chopped fresh cilantro, divided
   Salsa for topping
1/2 cup sour cream
6 Quesadillas (recipe at right)

Cover beans in water in a bowl and soak overnight. Drain. Cook red and green peppers and onion in 2 tablespoons of the olive oil over low heat in an 8-quart pot for 1 minute. Add soaked beans and sauté, stirring constantly, for 5 minutes. Add chicken stock, garlic, 2 teaspoons of the cumin and 2 teaspoons of the chili powder. Simmer, uncovered, for 1 hour and 10 minutes. Add more chicken broth as necessary. Stir in tomatoes. Simmer for 20 minutes or until the beans are done. Season with salt and pepper.

Crack the chicken breast bones to flatten. Rub breasts with remaining 2 tablespoons olive oil and season with remaining 1 teaspoon chili powder, remaining 1 teaspoon cumin, 1 tablespoon garlic and 2 tablespoons of the cilantro. Roast chicken in a preheated 350 degree oven for 30 minutes or until cooked through. Cool chicken slightly and remove meat from bones.

Place a generous portion of cooked beans in a large, flat soup bowl. Slice cooked chicken thinly, keeping skin on (skin may be removed, but some of the seasoning will be lost) and place on top of the beans. Garnish with salsa, sour cream, the remaining 4 tablespoons cilantro and a warm Quesadilla. *Yield: 6 servings*

★ *If desired, substitute chicken breasts with boneless skinless chicken breasts and grill for 5 to 7 minutes per side.*

## Quesadillas for White Bean Chicken Chili

6 flour tortillas
1 1/2 cups grated Cheddar cheese
12 tablespoons sour cream
   hot peppers to taste

Top each tortilla with 1/4 cup Cheddar cheese, 2 tablespoons sour cream and hot peppers to taste. Fold each tortilla into quarters. Warm in a preheated 350 degree oven. *Yield: 6 servings*

# Chicken Breasts with Bacon

*Decadent and delicious*

12 boneless, skinless chicken breasts
 8 ounces cream cheese
 6 green onions, chopped
24 slices bacon
 toothpicks

Flatten chicken breasts with a meat mallet until thin. Beat cream cheese and green onions and form into 12 walnut-sized pieces. Wrap a breast around each piece of cream cheese. Wrap 2 bacon slices around each bundle of chicken, covering as much of the chicken as possible. Secure with toothpicks. Place chicken bundles on a broiler pan and broil in a preheated broiler, turning occasionally, for 30 minutes or until bacon and chicken are well done. *Yield: 12 servings*

# Portobello Mushroom Chicken and Wild Rice

*Good for company*

1/2 cup sliced Portobello mushrooms
1/4 cup chopped onions
1/2 cup chopped artichoke hearts
 1 tablespoon olive oil
 1 cup cooked wild rice
 4 boneless, skinless chicken breasts
 garlic powder
 salt and pepper
 4 slices Swiss cheese
 kitchen string or toothpicks

Sauté mushrooms, onions and artichokes in olive oil over medium heat in a skillet. Add to cooked wild rice. Set aside.

Flatten chicken with a meat mallet until thin. Season with garlic powder, salt and pepper. Place 1 slice Swiss cheese on each chicken breast. Spread 1 1/2 to 2 teaspoons of the rice-mushroom mixture on top. Roll each chicken breast to enclose filling. Secure with kitchen string or toothpicks. Bake in a buttered 9x13-inch ovenproof baking dish in a preheated 350 degree oven for 30 minutes or until chicken is cooked through. *Yield: 4 servings*

# Chicken and Artichoke Casserole

*Easy to make ahead*

2 cups julienne cut carrots
1 cup chopped red pepper
1/3 cup chopped green onions
7 tablespoons butter, divided
6 tablespoons flour
1/2 teaspoon salt
1/4 teaspoon pepper
1 1/2 cups chicken broth
1 1/2 cups milk, divided
1/4 cup dry Sherry
4 cups cubed, cooked chicken
4 strips bacon, cooked and crumbled
1 1/2 cups shredded Mozzarella cheese
1 1/2 cups shredded sharp Cheddar cheese
1 can (14 ounces) artichoke hearts, drained
  and quartered
1/3 cup freshly grated Parmesan cheese
2 teaspoons chopped fresh parsley

Cook carrots, red pepper, and green onions in 1 tablespoon of the butter over medium-high heat in a skillet until crisp tender. Remove from heat and set aside.

Melt remaining 6 tablespoons butter over medium heat in a saucepan. Stir in flour, salt and pepper. Cook, stirring constantly, until smooth and bubbly. Gradually stir in chicken broth and 1 cup of the milk, stirring constantly for 3 to 5 minutes or until sauce thickens.

Stir together sauce, remaining 1/2 cup milk, Sherry, cooked chicken, crumbled bacon, Mozzarella cheese, Cheddar cheese and artichokes. Spoon mixture into a greased 9x13-inch ovenproof baking dish. Top with Parmesan cheese and parsley. Cover tightly with aluminum foil. Bake in a preheated 350 degree oven for 30 to 40 minutes. Uncover and bake an additional 20 minutes. *Yield: 12 servings*

★ *Serve with white or wild rice or over pasta. Casserole can be made 24 hours ahead, covered, refrigerated and baked an additional 10 minutes. Can also be frozen for up to 2 months in a casserole dish or resealable plastic freezer bags.*

*Cherry blossoms at the Jefferson Memorial.*

# Grilled Pork Tenderloin

*Delicious*

¹/2 cup soy sauce
¹/2 cup cream Sherry
2 tablespoons brown sugar
1 teaspoon ground ginger
2 cloves garlic, crushed
2 (³/4 pound) pork tenderloins

Combine soy sauce, Sherry, brown sugar, ginger, garlic and pork tenderloins in a resealable plastic bag. Marinate in the refrigerator for 8 hours or overnight.

Remove pork from marinade. Prepare a very hot grill. Grill pork for 12 to 15 minutes, turning once. Slice and serve immediately. *Yield: 4 to 6 servings*

★ *Marinade can be boiled and served as a sauce.*

# Sweet and Spicy Grilled Pork Chops

1 jalapeño, stemmed
1 chipotle chile, stemmed
3 large garlic cloves, peeled
5 tablespoons olive oil, divided
¹/4 cup soy sauce
2 tablespoons Dijon mustard
2 tablespoons honey
1 tablespoon sesame oil
1 tablespoon chopped fresh rosemary
2 teaspoons freshly grated lemon zest
4 (8 ounce) pork loin chops

Place jalapeño, chipotle chile and garlic in a small ovenproof baking dish. Drizzle with 1 tablespoon of the olive oil. Roast 40 minutes or until very soft in a preheated 350 degree oven. Cool and purée in food processor. Whisk remaining 4 tablespoons olive oil, soy sauce, Dijon mustard, honey, sesame oil, rosemary and lemon zest in a medium bowl. Pour marinade into a resealable plastic bag and add pork chops. Refrigerate 1 hour or overnight. Remove pork from marinade and grill over high heat about 10 minutes per side or until no longer pink in center. Can also broil in a preheated broiler for 10 minutes per side. *Yield: 4 servings*

# Pork with Pear Sauce

*Vary the pears to vary the taste*

4 (1/2-inch thick) boneless pork loin chops
1 teaspoon dried rubbed sage
1/2 teaspoon salt
1/4 teaspoon pepper
1/2 cup flour
2 tablespoons olive oil
3 large pears, peeled, cored and thinly sliced
1/2 cup dry white wine
1/2 cup chicken broth
2 tablespoons sugar
    salt and pepper

Season pork chops with sage, 1/2 teaspoon salt and 1/4 teaspoon pepper. Dust pork chops with flour. Sauté pork chops in olive oil over medium-high in a skillet for 3 to 4 minutes per side or until brown. Transfer to a plate and keep warm. Drain fat from skillet, add pears and sauté for 2 minutes. Add white wine, chicken broth and sugar. Increase heat and boil for 5 minutes or until pears are tender and syrup is thick. Return pork chops and any accumulated juices to skillet. Lower heat and simmer for 5 to 7 minutes or until pork chops are cooked through. Season with salt and pepper. Arrange pork chops on serving platter and top with pear sauce. Serve immediately. *Yield: 4 servings*

# Pork Tenderloins with Green Onion Sauce

*Appealing presentation*

1/4 cup soy sauce
1/4 cup Bourbon
2 tablespoons brown sugar
3 (3/4 pound) pork tenderloins
    Green Onion Sauce (recipe follows)

Combine soy sauce, Bourbon, brown sugar and pork in a resealable plastic bag. Marinate, turning occasionally, 2 hours or overnight in the refrigerator.

    Remove pork from marinade. Roast on a rack in a shallow roasting pan in a preheated 325 degree oven for 30 minutes or up to 1 hour to desired doneness. Baste occasionally with marinade. Slice in thin diagonal slices. Serve with Green Onion Sauce. *Yield: 5 to 6 servings*

★ *Pork tenderloins can also be grilled over medium-high heat for 15 to 20 minutes, basting and turning often.*

### Green Onion Sauce

1/2 cup sour cream
1/3 cup mayonnaise
1 tablespoon finely chopped green onions
1 tablespoon dry mustard
1 1/2 tablespoons vinegar
    salt

Combine sour cream, mayonnaise, green onions, dry mustard and vinegar in a mixing bowl. Season with salt. Refrigerate until ready to serve. *Yield: 3/4 cup*

★

# Beef with Fresh Asparagus

*Better than Chinese take-out*

1/2 pound flank steak
1 1/2 teaspoons soy sauce
2 1/2 teaspoons Sherry
1/2 teaspoon sesame oil
1/4 teaspoon ginger juice
2 1/2 teaspoons cornstarch, divided
3 tablespoons plus 1 teaspoon peanut oil
1/2 pound fresh asparagus
1 small carrot
2 slices ginger, shredded
1 tablespoon oyster sauce
1/2 teaspoon sugar
1 teaspoon wine
1/2 cup beef broth
1 teaspoon cold water

Slice flank steak across the grain into 1 1/2x2-inch slices. Place in a resealable plastic bag. Combine soy sauce, Sherry, sesame oil, ginger juice, 1 1/2 teaspoons of the cornstarch and 1 teaspoon of the peanut oil in a mixing bowl. Pour over flank steak. Refrigerate for 2 hours or longer. Break off tough ends of the asparagus spears and cut diagonally into 2-inch pieces. Cut carrot on the diagonal.

Heat the remaining 3 tablespoons peanut oil over high heat in a wok. Add ginger and stir fry for 30 seconds. Add marinated flank steak and stir fry 2 minutes or until redness disappears. Remove flank steak and set aside. Stir fry carrots and asparagus in the wok for 30 seconds. Add oyster sauce, sugar, wine and beef broth. Cook for 3 minutes. Return flank steak to wok. Combine the remaining 1 teaspoon cornstarch and water in a mixing bowl. Add to wok to thicken sauce. Serve immediately. *Yield: 4 servings*

# Tenderloin Roast Stuffed with Pâté

*Perfect for a dinner party*

1/2 cup Pâté de Campagne
2 pounds tenderloin roast
3 tablespoons olive oil, divided
4 cloves garlic
3 sprigs fresh rosemary

Work pâté into a paste. Insert knife through the middle of the tenderloin roast and gently turn without removing any meat. Stuff center with pâté. Rub roast with 1 tablespoon of the olive oil. Sauté garlic and rosemary sprigs in remaining 2 tablespoons olive oil in a skillet. Add roast and brown on all sides. Place roast in a large baking pan lined with parchment paper. Cook in a preheated 350 degree oven for 20 minutes. *Yield: 4 to 6 servings*

# Filet Mignon with Shallot Sauce

*Meat aficionados will rave*

12 ounces shallots, halved
2 tablespoons olive oil
1/4 cup sugar
1/2 cup balsamic vinegar
1 cup chicken broth
1 cup beef broth
2 tablespoons chopped fresh thyme
  salt and pepper
4 (8 ounces each) filet mignon steaks

Sauté shallots in olive oil over medium heat in a skillet for 15 minutes. Sprinkle with sugar and stir for 5 minutes or until shallots are golden brown. Add vinegar and boil for 1 minute or until reduced to syrup consistency. Add chicken and beef broths and boil 10 minutes or until liquid is reduced to sauce consistency. Add thyme. Season with salt and pepper. Can be prepared 1 day ahead. Cover and chill. Reheat before serving.

Prepare grill or preheat broiler. Season steaks with salt and pepper. Grill or broil steaks 5 minutes per side for medium-rare or longer to achieve desired doneness. Spoon warm shallot sauce around steaks to serve. *Yield: 4 servings*

# Stuffed Boneless Rib Roast

*Gorgonzola and garlic make this special*

    4 pound boneless rib roast
  1/4 to 1/2 pound Gorgonzola cheese
    6 garlic cloves, chopped
      pepper
  1/4 cup olive oil
    4 sprigs fresh rosemary
    1 cup red wine
    2 shallots, chopped
    2 tablespoons butter
      kitchen string

Stuff center of rib roast with Gorgonzola cheese. Rub the outside of roast with chopped garlic and ground pepper. Tie roast with kitchen string to hold Gorgonzola in place.

Heat olive oil in an 8-quart pot. Add rib roast and brown all sides of the meat. Do not turn meat until roast easily comes away from skillet.

Place browned roast in an ovenproof baking dish and cover with fresh rosemary sprigs. Bake in a preheated 350 degree oven for 20 minutes or until done. The meat should be red to pink inside.

While roast is cooking, boil red wine and chopped shallots over medium heat in a saucepan until reduced. Add butter and stir until melted. Pour on a serving platter and place the cooked roast in the center. Decorate with rosemary sprigs.
*Yield: 6 to 8 servings*

★ *Gorgonzola is a mild Italian blue cheese available at gourmet grocery stores or specialty shops.*

# Asian Flank Steak

*A taste of the Orient*

  1/4 cup soy sauce
  1/4 cup Worcestershire sauce
    2 tablespoons fresh lemon juice
    2 tablespoons chopped fresh cilantro
    1 tablespoon minced fresh ginger
1 1/4 pounds flank steak, fat trimmed

Combine soy sauce, Worcestershire sauce, lemon juice, cilantro, ginger and flank steak in a resealable plastic bag. Marinate, turning occasionally, for 1 hour at room temperature or refrigerate overnight.

Prepare grill or preheat broiler. Grill or broil flank steak for 5 minutes per side for rare or longer to achieve desired doneness. Transfer to a serving platter. Let stand for 10 minutes.

Drain marinade into a saucepan and boil for 3 minutes. Thinly slice steak across the grain. Serve with sauce. *Yield: 4 servings*

★ *Marinade is also great with tuna steak.*

# Individual Beef Wellingtons

*Impressive entrée*

8 ounces fresh mushrooms, sliced
1 tablespoon minced shallot
1 teaspoon chopped fresh parsley
2 tablespoons butter, melted
3 cups shredded Gruyère cheese
8 to 12 ounces rare roast beef, julienne cut
2 tablespoons prepared horseradish
6 puff pastry sheets, cut into 6-inch squares
1 egg, beaten with 1 teaspoon water
   Horseradish Sauce (recipe at right)

Sauté mushrooms, shallot and parsley in butter over medium-high heat in a skillet for 3 to 4 minutes. Drain well and cool.

Combine cheese, roast beef, horseradish and cooked mushroom mixture in a large mixing bowl.

Place 1 puff pastry square on a work surface and spoon 1/6 of the filling into the center of the pastry. Fold up corners of pastry, pinching to seal. Transfer to an ungreased baking sheet, seam side down. Repeat with remaining puff pastry squares. Brush filled pastries with beaten egg mixture.

Bake in a preheated 425 degree oven for 25 to 30 minutes or until puffed and golden. Serve immediately with Horseradish Sauce. *Yield: 6 servings*

★ *Stuffed pastries can be made ahead and refrigerated until ready to bake. When time is short, deli roast beef may be substituted.*

Horseradish Sauce
1 1/2 cups sour cream
 1/4 cup prepared horseradish
 1/4 teaspoon minced fresh garlic

Combine ingredients in a mixing bowl. Refrigerate until ready to use. *Yield: 1 3/4 cups*

## Veal Piccata

*Italian paradise*

24 thin slices veal, 1 to 1¹/2 pounds
    salt and pepper
 1 cup flour
 8 tablespoons butter
 2 lemons, juiced
¹/4 cup white wine
 1 cup chicken broth
    fresh parsley to garnish

Pound veal very thin between two pieces of wax paper. Season with salt and pepper. Dredge through flour. Sauté veal, in batches, in 2 tablespoons of the butter over medium heat, adding butter as needed. Transfer veal to a plate. Tent with aluminum foil to keep warm. Add lemon juice, wine and chicken broth to same skillet. Cover and simmer for 10 minutes. Return veal to skillet to reheat. Garnish with fresh parsley. Serve ladled with sauce. *Yield: 6 servings*

## Veal Chops with Mushrooms

*For the mushroom lover*

 4 veal chops
    salt and pepper
¹/4 cup flour
 2 tablespoons butter
12 ounces fresh mushrooms, sliced
 2 tablespoons chopped shallots
¹/2 cup white wine
¹/2 cup whipping cream
 1 tablespoon Cognac

Season veal with salt and pepper. Dredge veal in flour. Sauté in butter over medium heat in a skillet for 10 minutes. Turn veal chops and cook an additional 10 minutes. Transfer to a serving platter and tent with aluminum foil to keep warm.

Sauté mushrooms in same skillet over high heat, stirring constantly, for 2 minutes. Season with salt and pepper. Add shallots and cook for 1 minute, stirring constantly. Add wine. Cook until wine is almost evaporated. Lower heat. Add cream and simmer for 5 minutes or until thick and golden. Pour any juices from the veal into the sauce. Add Cognac and stir. Pour sauce over veal chops. Serve immediately. *Yield: 4 servings*

## Marinated Roast Loin of Veal

*Port wine and oranges add flavor*

1 bottle (1 liter) Port wine
3 medium oranges, juiced and finely zested
1 cup coarsely chopped fresh basil
2 to 3 pounds veal tip roast, butterflied
   salt and pepper
1 cup veal or chicken broth
   kitchen string

Combine Port wine, orange juice, orange zest, basil and veal in a resealable plastic bag. Season with salt and pepper. Marinate in refrigerator for 24 hours.

Remove veal roast from marinade. Roll and tie veal securely with kitchen string. Bake on a rack in a shallow roasting pan in a preheated 350 degree oven for $1^1/4$ hours or until meat thermometer inserted in center of roast registers 140 degrees. Remove from oven. Rest veal for 10 minutes with an aluminum foil tent loosely over it.

While roast is cooking, strain and boil 3 cups of the marinade in a saucepan for 20 minutes or until reduced to $1^1/2$ cups. Add veal or chicken stock and cook over medium-high heat for 12 additional minutes or until the sauce is reduced to 1 cup and slightly thick. Season with salt and pepper.

Slice veal roast about $^1/2$ inch thick. Drizzle with sauce. *Yield: 6 to 8 servings*

## Grilled Quail with Rosemary

*A change of pace*

8 quail
$^1/4$ cup olive oil
   salt and pepper
2 to 3 tablespoons fresh chopped rosemary

Place each quail, breast side down, with tail facing you. Use kitchen shears to cut along one side of backbone down entire length. With breast side still down, turn quail so the neck faces you. Cut along other side of backbone. Remove backbone. Flip quail so breast side is now up and open on cutting board. Flatten bird with hand, if necessary.

Brush both sides of each quail with olive oil. Season with salt and pepper. Sprinkle rosemary on each quail breast.

Prepare a hot grill. Grease grill with olive or vegetable oil.

Cook quail, breast side up, for 4 minutes. Turn quail over. Cook for an additional 4 minutes. Serve immediately. *Yield: 4 servings*

# Grilled Rosemary Lamb Chops

*Wonderful and easy*

3/4 cup balsamic vinegar
6 tablespoons olive oil
3 tablespoons fresh lemon juice
3 tablespoons minced fresh rosemary
6 cloves garlic, minced
1 teaspoon black pepper
12 (1-inch thick) loin lamb chops, fat trimmed

Combine balsamic vinegar, olive oil, lemon juice, rosemary, garlic, pepper and lamb chops in a resealable plastic bag. Marinate, turning occasionally, for 4 hours in the refrigerator.

Prepare a very hot grill. Grill lamb chops, basting often with marinade, for 4 minutes per side for medium-rare or longer to desired doneness.
*Yield: 4 servings*

★ *If fresh rosemary is unavailable, use 1 tablespoon dried rosemary.*

# Grilled Lamb with Apricot Marinade

*A lamb lover's favorite*

3/4 cup apricot nectar
1/4 cup soy sauce
1/4 cup white wine
3 tablespoons Worcestershire sauce
1 clove garlic, crushed
   butterflied leg of lamb, fat trimmed

Combine apricot nectar, soy sauce, white wine, Worcestershire sauce, garlic and lamb in a resealable plastic bag. Marinate for 8 hours or overnight in refrigerator.

Grill or broil for 8 minutes on each side for medium-rare meat or longer to achieve desired doneness. *Yield: 8 servings*

Pasta and Pizza

★

# Pasta and Pizza

★

*Penne with Salmon and Broccoli.*

# Penne with Salmon and Broccoli

*This dish needs only a glass of wine and crusty bread*

1 quart water
2 tablespoons lemon juice
12 ounces fresh salmon fillets
12 ounces penne pasta
1/4 cup chopped shallots
2 cloves garlic, crushed
1 tablespoon olive oil
1 tablespoon butter
2 roasted red peppers, julienne cut
2 roasted yellow peppers, julienne cut
2 cups broccoli florets or snow peas
3/4 cup heavy cream
1/4 cup dry white wine
1 1/2 teaspoons Dijon mustard
   pinch of nutmeg
   salt and pepper
1 tablespoon chopped fresh dill
1/2 cup chopped fresh parsley
1/2 cup toasted pine nuts
1/4 cup freshly grated Parmesan cheese

Heat water and lemon juice until boiling in a skillet. Reduce heat and poach salmon for 10 minutes. Remove with a slotted spoon and cool. Flake salmon into 3/4-inch pieces.

Prepare penne according to package directions and drain.

Sauté shallots and garlic in olive oil and butter over medium-high heat in a skillet until tender. Add roasted red and yellow peppers and broccoli. Cook on low heat for 2 to 3 minutes or until vegetables are heated through, yet remain crisp. Slowly add cream, white wine, Dijon mustard and nutmeg. Season with salt and pepper. Boil and reduce heat. Add salmon. Cook for 1 to 2 additional minutes or until salmon is heated through.

Pour sauce over cooked penne. Sprinkle dill, parsley and pine nuts on top and gently mix. Garnish with Parmesan cheese. Serve immediately.
*Yield: 4 servings*

★ *Roast peppers in a lightly oiled baking pan in a preheated 450 degree oven, turning occasionally, for 25 minutes or until evenly blistered. Place peppers in a paper bag, and seal. When cool, peel skins, and remove core and seeds.*

# Asian Chicken Fettuccine

*Wonderful fresh flavors*

4 boneless, skinless chicken breasts
1 green onion, minced
3 cloves garlic, minced
1/3 cup hoisin sauce
2 teaspoons sesame oil
2 tablespoons soy sauce
1 tablespoon sugar
1/2 teaspoon salt
1/4 teaspoon pepper
1/2 cup small broccoli florets
1/2 cup fresh snow peas
2 carrots, julienne cut
1/2 red pepper, julienne cut
1/2 yellow pepper, julienne cut
2 green onions, sliced
1 tablespoon olive oil
1 tablespoon butter
1 package (9 ounces) fresh fettuccine
2 tablespoons chopped fresh cilantro
  Sesame Ginger Dressing (recipe at right)

Rinse chicken and pat dry. Process onion and garlic in a food processor until finely minced. Add hoisin sauce, sesame oil, soy sauce, sugar, salt and pepper, and mix well. Spread mixture on chicken in a dish, and marinate in the refrigerator for 1 hour or longer. Place chicken on a baking sheet, and broil for 7 to 10 minutes per side. Cool slightly, and slice thinly.

Blanch broccoli and snow peas; drain well. Sauté carrots, red and yellow peppers and green onions in olive oil and butter over medium heat in a skillet until tender but crisp. Prepare fettuccine according to package directions. Drain. Toss fettuccine, vegetables, cilantro and chicken with Sesame Ginger Dressing in a serving bowl. Serve immediately. *Yield: 4 servings*

★ *Garnish with 1 tablespoon toasted sesame seeds if desired.*

Sesame Ginger Dressing
2 tablespoons vegetable oil
2 tablespoons rice wine vinegar
3 tablespoons soy sauce
1 tablespoons ginger tamari
2 teaspoons sesame oil
1 teaspoon sugar
1 teaspoon grated fresh ginger
1 teaspoon minced garlic
  salt and pepper

Combine first 8 ingredients in a mixing bowl, and mix well. Season with salt and pepper. *Yield: 2/3 cup*

# Pasta Florentine

*Surprisingly delicious*

8 ounces thin spaghetti
1/2 cup butter, melted
1 package (10 ounces) frozen spinach
4 cups shredded Monterey Jack cheese
1/4 cup finely diced onion
2 cups sliced fresh mushrooms
1/2 teaspoon oregano
    salt and pepper
16 ounces sour cream
1 1/2 cups freshly grated Parmesan cheese

Break spaghetti into thirds. Prepare according to package directions. Drain well. Toss spaghetti with melted butter. Thaw and drain spinach. Add spinach, Monterey Jack cheese, onion and mushrooms to spaghetti. Toss well. Add oregano and season with salt and pepper. Stir in sour cream. Transfer to a greased 9x13-inch ovenproof baking dish. Sprinkle with Parmesan cheese. Bake, uncovered, in a preheated 350 degree oven for 35 minutes. *Yield: 4 to 6 servings*

★ *Great to make ahead.*

# Rigatoni with Sausage, Ricotta and Basil

1 pound rigatoni
1/2 yellow onion, chopped
2 tablespoons butter
3/4 pound sweet or hot bulk sausage
1 1/2 cups chopped canned tomatoes
    salt and pepper
1/2 cup Ricotta cheese
2 tablespoons torn fresh basil
2 tablespoons freshly grated Parmesan cheese

Prepare rigatoni according to package directions. Drain and set aside.

Sauté onion in butter over medium heat in a saucepan for 3 to 4 minutes. Add sausage and brown. Drain fat. Add tomatoes. Season with salt and pepper. Combine sauce and cooked rigatoni in a mixing bowl. Add Ricotta cheese and basil. Toss until well mixed. Transfer to a serving bowl. Garnish with Parmesan cheese. Serve immediately. *Yield: 6 servings*

# Asparagus and Onion Lasagna

*Great with Vidalia onions*

6 cups thinly sliced sweet onions
8 tablespoons butter, divided
   salt and pepper
1/2 cup white wine
1 pound asparagus, cut into 1-inch pieces
1/2 cup flour
2 1/2 cups milk
1 1/2 cups freshly grated Parmesan cheese, divided
1 package (8 ounces) no-boil lasagna noodles
2 cups shredded Mozzarella cheese

Sauté onions in 2 tablespoons of the butter over medium heat in a skillet, stirring occasionally, for 15 minutes or until tender. Season with salt and pepper. Add white wine. Cook for an additional 5 minutes. Transfer to a separate bowl.

Sauté asparagus in 2 tablespoons of the butter over medium heat in the same skillet until just tender. Set aside.

Melt the remaining 4 tablespoons butter over medium heat in a saucepan. Add flour and cook, stirring constantly, for 3 minutes. Whisk milk in slowly and boil. Season with salt and pepper. Add 1 cup of the Parmesan cheese. Simmer sauce for 2 to 4 minutes or until sauce thickens.

Spread 1/2 cup sauce on bottom of a greased 9x13-inch ovenproof baking dish. Layer 4 of the lasagna noodles, 1/2 of the cooked onions, 1/2 of the asparagus, 2/3 cup of the Mozzarella and 1 cup of the sauce in the prepared baking dish. Repeat layers. Top with 4 lasagna noodles, the remaining sauce, the remaining Mozzarella and the remaining Parmesan cheese. Bake in a preheated 375 degree oven for 25 to 30 minutes or until golden. Let stand 10 minutes before serving. *Yield: 6 to 8 servings*

★ *No-boil lasagna noodles are available in most gourmet grocery stores. If not available, substitute conventional lasagna noodles prepared according to package directions. If asparagus is not in season, substitute thinly sliced green zucchini.*

# Chicken Florentine Lasagna

*Speedy and unique*

2 packages (10 ounces) frozen chopped
  spinach
3 cups chopped cooked chicken
2 cups shredded Cheddar cheese
1/3 cup chopped onion
1/2 teaspoon grated nutmeg
1 tablespoon cornstarch
1/2 teaspoon salt
1/4 teaspoon pepper
1 tablespoon soy sauce
1 can (10 3/4 ounces) cream of mushroom
  soup
8 ounces sour cream
1 jar (4 1/2 ounces) sliced mushrooms, drained
1/3 cup mayonnaise
6 no-boil lasagna noodles
1 cup freshly grated Parmesan cheese
1 cup chopped pecans
2 tablespoons butter, melted

Thaw and drain frozen spinach. Combine spinach, chicken, Cheddar cheese, onion, nutmeg, cornstarch, salt, pepper, soy sauce, cream of mushroom soup, sour cream, mushrooms and mayonnaise in a mixing bowl. Stir well. Spread 3/4 cup of the chicken mixture in a lightly greased 9x13-inch ovenproof baking dish. Top with 3 lasagna noodles. Spread half the remaining chicken mixture over noodles. Repeat with the remaining noodles and chicken mixture. Sprinkle with Parmesan cheese.

Sauté pecans in butter over medium heat in a skillet for 3 minutes or until toasted. Sprinkle over casserole.

Cover and bake in a preheated 350 degree oven for 55 to 60 minutes. Let stand 5 minutes before serving. *Yield: 8 servings*

# Spinach Lasagna with Shrimp

*An elegant entrée*

4 pounds medium shrimp, cooked and
  cleaned
2 medium onions, chopped
8 tablespoons butter
5 tablespoons flour
  salt and pepper
1 tablespoon curry powder
2 quarts half and half
2 pounds fresh green spinach lasagna noodles
2 cups freshly grated Asiago or
  Parmesan cheese
  Paprika to garnish

Cut shrimp lengthwise. Sauté onions in butter in a saucepan until translucent. Stir in flour, and cook until mixture is a thick paste. Season with salt and pepper. Add curry powder and half and half. Stir constantly until sauce is thickened.

Layer 1/4 cup of sauce on bottom of a greased 9x13-inch ovenproof baking dish. Alternate layers of lasagna, shrimp and sauce, ending with 1 cup of the sauce for the top. Sprinkle with Asiago or Parmesan cheese and lightly dust with paprika. Bake in a preheated 375 degree oven for 45 minutes or until bubbling. *Yield: 10 to 12 servings*

# Chicken Pecan Fettuccine

*Toasted pecans add crunch*

1 pound boneless, skinless chicken breasts
3/4 cup butter, melted, divided
3 cups sliced fresh mushrooms
1 cup sliced green onions with tops
3/4 teaspoon salt, divided
1/2 teaspoon pepper, divided
1/2 teaspoon garlic powder, divided
10 ounces fettuccine
1 egg yolk
2/3 cup half and half
2 tablespoons chopped fresh parsley
1/2 cup freshly grated Parmesan cheese
1 cup chopped pecans, toasted

Cut chicken into 1-inch pieces. Sauté chicken in 1/4 cup of the melted butter in a skillet until lightly browned. Remove chicken. Set aside, keeping warm. Sauté mushrooms, green onions, 1/2 teaspoon of the salt, 1/4 teaspoon of the pepper and 1/4 teaspoon of the garlic powder in the same skillet until tender. Return chicken to skillet. Simmer for 10 minutes or until chicken is done.

Prepare fettuccine according to package directions. Drain fettuccine and return to pot. Whisk egg yolk and half and half in a mixing bowl. Add to cooked fettuccine. Add remaining 1/2 cup melted butter, parsley, the remaining 1/4 teaspoon salt, the remaining 1/4 teaspoon pepper and the remaining 1/4 teaspoon garlic powder. Cook, stirring constantly, until bubbly. Add Parmesan cheese, tossing until mixed well. Add chicken mixture and toss. To serve, arrange pasta on a platter and sprinkle with toasted pecans. *Yield: 0 servings*

# Artichoke Linguine

*Tangy and tasty*

4 tablespoons butter
6 tablespoons olive oil, divided
2 tablespoons flour
1 cup chicken broth
1 clove garlic, minced
1 tablespoon chopped fresh parsley
1 tablespoon lemon juice
   salt and pepper
2 cans (6 ounces) artichoke hearts, drained and chopped
1/2 pound linguine
1/4 cup freshly grated Parmesan cheese

Melt butter and 4 tablespoons of the olive oil over medium heat in a skillet. Stir in flour. Add chicken broth and simmer, stirring constantly, for 1 minute or until thick. Reduce heat. Add garlic, parsley and lemon juice. Season with salt and pepper. Cook, stirring occasionally, for 5 minutes. Add artichokes. Cover and simmer for 8 minutes. Prepare pasta according to package directions. Drain, and return to pot. Add remaining 2 tablespoons olive oil, Parmesan cheese and artichoke sauce to pasta and toss well. *Yield: 4 servings*

# Pasta with Asparagus and Sun-Dried Tomatoes

*A refreshing spring dish*

1 pound fusilli
3 garlic cloves, minced
2 tablespoons olive oil
2 cups sliced mixed wild mushrooms
8 ounces asparagus, cut into 1-inch pieces
1/2 cup sun-dried tomatoes, (not oil-packed) julienne-cut
1/2 cup dry white wine
1/2 cup whipping cream
1/4 cup Mascarpone cheese or cream cheese
1 tablespoon chopped fresh parsley
salt and pepper
1/4 cup freshly grated Parmesan cheese

Prepare fusilli according to package directions. Drain and set aside. Sauté garlic in olive oil over medium-high heat in a skillet for 1 minute or until golden. Add mushrooms, asparagus and sun-dried tomatoes. Sauté for 10 minutes or until liquid evaporates. Add wine. Boil for 3 minutes or until liquid is reduced by half. Add cream, Mascarpone cheese and parsley. Simmer for 8 minutes or until liquid is reduced to sauce consistency. Season with salt and pepper. Remove from heat. Toss sauce and fusilli to coat. Sprinkle with Parmesan cheese. Serve immediately. *Yield: 6 servings*

★ *Substitute fusilli with rotini or penne. Use assorted wild mushrooms such as Cremini, Shiitake or Portobello.*

# Thick and Hearty Spaghetti Sauce

1 pound ground beef
2 cups coarsely chopped onions
3 cloves garlic, minced
1 pound sweet Italian sausage
1/4 cup water
2 cans (14 1/2 ounces) Italian-style stewed tomatoes
1 can (29 ounces) tomato sauce
2 bay leaves
1 teaspoon dried oregano
1/2 teaspoon dried basil
1 teaspoon dried rosemary
1/2 teaspoon dried marjoram
salt and pepper
Tabasco (optional)
10 large fresh mushrooms, sliced
1 green pepper, chopped
1/4 cup chopped fresh parsley
1/4 teaspoon chopped fresh cilantro (optional)
1/2 cup dry red wine
3 ounces tomato paste

Brown ground beef over medium heat in a skillet and drain. Add onions. Reduce heat and simmer until onions are glossy. Stir in garlic. Set aside.

Cook sweet Italian sausage in 1/4 cup water over medium heat in a skillet until almost done. Slice sausage into 1/2-inch pieces and add to the cooked ground beef. Add tomatoes, tomato sauce, bay leaves, oregano, basil, rosemary and marjoram. Season with salt and pepper. Add Tabasco, if desired. Simmer tomato mixture over low heat for 35 to 45 minutes. Add mushrooms, green pepper and parsley, and check seasonings. Add cilantro, if desired. Add red wine. Simmer, covered, over low heat for 1 hour. Add tomato paste and bring to a low boil. Serve over cooked spaghetti or other pasta. *Yield: 8 to 10 servings*

★

## Szechuan Noodles with Peanut Sauce

*A pasta with an Asian flavor*

12 ounces spaghetti or linguine
1/3 cup hot water
1/3 cup smooth peanut butter
2 teaspoons soy sauce
2 teaspoons rice vinegar
8 tablespoons chopped green onions, divided
2 cloves garlic, minced
1 teaspoon sugar
1/4 teaspoon red pepper flakes

Cook pasta according to package directions. Drain well. Blend hot water and peanut butter in a mixing bowl. Add soy sauce, rice vinegar, 7 tablespoons of the green onions, garlic, sugar and red pepper flakes. Mix well. Toss sauce with the pasta in a heated serving bowl. Garnish with the remaining 1 tablespoon green onions. *Yield: 6 to 8 servings*

★ *Use additional red pepper for a spicier pasta.*

## Ziti with Spinach

*Wilted spinach makes this dish special*

1 medium white onion, chopped
3 garlic cloves, minced
2 tablespoons olive oil
1 can (28 ounces) chopped plum tomatoes
1/4 teaspoon crushed red pepper flakes
2 teaspoons dried oregano
salt and pepper
1 pound ziti
1 pound fresh spinach
8 ounces Mozzarella cheese, cut into
1/2-inch cubes
1 cup freshly grated Parmesan cheese, divided

Cook onion and garlic in olive oil over medium heat in a skillet for 5 minutes or until onion is softened. Add undrained chopped tomatoes, red pepper flakes and oregano. Increase heat, and boil the sauce, stirring occasionally, for 10 minutes or until most of the liquid evaporates. Season with salt and pepper.

Cook pasta according to package directions. Drain well and return to pot. Set aside. While pasta is cooking, thoroughly wash spinach, remove stems and coarsely chop. Stir tomato sauce, spinach, Mozzarella cheese and 1/3 cup of the Parmesan cheese into the pasta. Transfer mixture to a 9x13-inch greased ovenproof baking dish, and sprinkle with the remaining Parmesan cheese. Broil in a preheated broiler for 4 to 5 minutes or until Mozzarella begins to melt and turn golden. Serve immediately. *Yield: 8 servings*

★

## Pasta with Sun-Dried Tomatoes and Chicken

12 ounces rotini
 4 boneless, skinless chicken breasts
 1 clove garlic, crushed
 1 teaspoon dried basil
 1 teaspoon dried oregano
 1 teaspoon garlic powder
 1 teaspoon salt
 2 tablespoons oil from sun-dried tomato jar
 1 cup oil-packed, julienne-cut sun-dried
   tomatoes
 1/2 cup freshly grated Parmesan cheese

Prepare rotini according to package instructions. Drain and set aside. Cut chicken into 1-inch pieces. Sauté chicken, garlic, basil, oregano, garlic powder and salt in 2 tablespoons sun-dried tomato oil in a skillet for 5 to 7 minutes or until chicken loses pink color. Drain sun-dried tomatoes and add to skillet. Reduce heat and sauté for 3 minutes. Toss chicken mixture with pasta. Top with Parmesan cheese. Serve immediately. *Yield: 4 to 6 servings*

## Fettuccine with Shrimp

*A light, refreshing meal*

 8 ounces fettuccine or spinach fettuccine
 2 cups sliced fresh mushrooms
 1 cup chopped onion
 2 cloves garlic, minced
 2 tablespoons olive oil
 1/3 cup dry white wine
 1 cup chicken broth
 1 tablespoon fresh oregano
 1 tablespoon cornstarch
12 ounces large shrimp, peeled and deveined
 3/4 pound asparagus, cut into 2-inch pieces
 2 medium tomatoes, peeled, seeded
   and chopped
 1/4 cup freshly grated Parmesan cheese
 1/4 cup chopped fresh parsley

Prepare fettuccine according to package directions. Drain and set aside. Sauté mushrooms, onion and garlic in olive oil over medium heat in a deep skillet until translucent. Combine wine, chicken broth, oregano and cornstarch in a mixing bowl. Add to onion mixture. Cook until bubbly. Add shrimp and asparagus, cover, and simmer for 2 minutes or until shrimp turns pink and asparagus is crisp and tender. Stir in tomatoes, and heat through. Toss shrimp mixture, fettuccine, Parmesan cheese and parsley in a serving bowl. Serve hot. *Yield: 6 servings*

★

## Pasta Shells with Tomatoes and Olives

*Perfect for a picnic or pool party*

1/2 pound dried small pasta shells
1 tablespoon white wine vinegar
1 tablespoon vegetable oil
1 cup pitted ripe black olives, sliced
1 pint cherry tomatoes, quartered
1 small green pepper, chopped
1/2 cup thinly sliced celery
1/2 cup thinly sliced green onions
1/3 cup shredded fresh basil
2/3 cup mayonnaise
1 tablespoon fresh lemon juice
2 tablespoons water
   salt and pepper

Prepare pasta according to package directions. Drain and rinse under cold water. Toss with vinegar and vegetable oil in a serving bowl. Add olives, tomatoes, green pepper, celery, green onions, and basil. Whisk mayonnaise, lemon juice and water together in a separate mixing bowl. Pour dressing over pasta, and toss gently until well mixed. Season with salt and pepper. Cover and chill. Toss again before serving. *Yield: 0 servings*

★ *Recipe may be made up to 2 days in advance.*

## Potomac Pasta Salad

8 ounces bowtie pasta
3 firm tomatoes, peeled and quartered
1/2 pound fresh Mozzarella, cut into
   1/4-inch cubes
1 clove garlic, minced
12 fresh basil leaves, finely chopped
1 small red onion, sliced into rings
1/2 cup bottled Caesar salad dressing
   salt and pepper

Prepare pasta according to package directions. Drain, cool and place in a serving bowl. Add tomatoes, Mozzarella cheese, garlic, basil and onion. Toss well. Add Caesar salad dressing and toss until ingredients are well coated. Add more dressing if desired. Season with salt and pepper. Chill for 1/2 hour before serving. *Yield: 6 to 8 servings*

# Loughborough Pizza

*Washingtonians love the chicken and pine nuts*

3/4 cup sliced green onions, divided
4 cloves garlic, minced
4 tablespoons white vinegar
4 tablespoons reduced sodium soy sauce
4 tablespoons olive oil, divided
1 teaspoon crushed red pepper flakes
1/2 teaspoon black pepper
4 boneless, skinless chicken breasts
1 tablespoon cornstarch
1 red pepper, julienne-cut
1 (12-inch) pre-baked pizza crust
1/2 cup shredded Cheddar cheese
1/2 cup shredded Mozzarella cheese
1/4 cup sliced green onions
2 tablespoons pine nuts, toasted

Combine 1/2 cup of the green onions, garlic, vinegar, soy sauce, 2 tablespoons of the olive oil, red pepper flakes and black pepper in a mixing bowl or resealable plastic bag. Cut chicken into 1-inch pieces, and add to marinade. Refrigerate overnight.

Drain chicken and reserve marinade in a mixing bowl. Stir cornstarch into marinade. Cook marinated chicken in 2 tablespoons heated olive oil in a medium skillet for 3 minutes or until chicken loses pink color. Remove chicken from skillet, and keep warm.

Sauté red pepper in the same skillet until soft. Remove red pepper, and set aside. Heat marinade in the same skillet until thick and bubbly.

Spread thickened marinade on pizza crust. Sprinkle Cheddar and Mozzarella cheeses on top. Add chicken and sautéed red pepper. Place pizza directly on oven rack. Bake in a preheated 400 degree oven for 12 minutes. Top pizza with remaining 1/4 cup green onions and pine nuts. Bake for an additional 2 minutes. Serve immediately.
*Yield: 4 to 6 servings*

*Loughborough Pizza.*

# Wild Mushroom and Pesto Pizza

*A wonderful combination of flavors*

3 cups sliced wild fresh mushrooms
2 garlic cloves, minced
3 tablespoons olive oil
1/2 batch Pizza Dough (recipe at right)
1/2 cup prepared basil pesto
1 cup shredded Fontina cheese
2 tablespoons chopped fresh flat-leaf parsley
4 tablespoons freshly grated Parmesan cheese

Sauté mushrooms and garlic in olive oil over medium-high heat in a skillet for 10 minutes. Set aside.

Form Pizza Dough into a 12-inch circle. Transfer to a pizza pan, round baking sheet or a well-floured pizza peel.

Spread basil pesto on Pizza Dough, leaving a 1-inch border. Cover pesto with Fontina cheese. Top with cooked mushrooms. Sprinkle with parsley and Parmesan cheese.

Bake pizza in a preheated 500 degree oven for 15 to 20 minutes or until golden brown. Let stand 5 minutes. Slice and serve. *Yield: 4 to 6 servings*

★ *Shiitake, Cremini, Portobello and other wild mushrooms give this pizza an exotic taste.*

## Pizza Dough

1 package active dry yeast
1 cup warm water
2 1/2 cups flour, divided
1 tablespoon olive oil
1/2 teaspoon salt

Combine yeast and warm water in a mixing bowl. Stir in 1 1/2 cups of the flour. Add the remaining flour, olive oil and salt. Stir until just combined. Knead dough on floured surface for 5 minutes, adding more flour if the dough becomes too sticky. Transfer dough to a lightly oiled mixing bowl, and cover with a kitchen towel or cheesecloth. Let dough sit in a warm place (e.g., 100 degree oven) for 1 hour or until dough doubles in size. Divide pizza dough in half. Cover and let sit for 15 additional minutes. *Yield: 2 (12-inch) pizza crusts*

★ *This recipe can be used with any other pizza recipe in the chapter.*

## Pizza with Roasted Red Pepper Sauce

3 roasted red peppers, peeled and seeded
1 teaspoon balsamic vinegar
  salt and pepper
2 large leeks, white parts only
1 clove garlic, finely chopped
1 tablespoon olive oil
1/2 recipe Pizza Dough (see page 108)
  garlic oil
8 Niçoise olives, pitted and coarsely chopped
1 1/4 cups shredded Fontina cheese
3/4 cup shredded Provolone cheese
3 tablespoons freshly grated Parmesan cheese
2 teaspoons chopped Italian parsley

Purée roasted red peppers and balsamic vinegar. Season with salt and pepper. Set aside. Thinly slice leeks and cut in half. Sauté leeks and garlic in olive oil over medium heat in a skillet for 8 minutes or until tender. Season with salt and pepper.

Roll out Pizza Dough into a 12-inch circle and brush with garlic oil. Place on a lightly-oiled pizza pan or a well-floured wooden peel. Spread 2/3 cup of the red pepper sauce over dough, reserving the remaining red pepper sauce for another purpose. Cover with cooked leeks and chopped olives. Toss Fontina and Provolone cheeses together. Sprinkle on top of pizza.

Bake in a preheated 500 degree oven for 8 to 12 minutes or until the crust is golden and crisp. Sprinkle with Parmesan cheese and parsley. Serve immediately. *Yield: 4 to 6 servings*

★ *A pre-baked pizza crust can be used instead of homemade pizza dough. The remaining red pepper sauce can be tossed with pasta.*

## Zesty White Pizza

1 clove garlic, minced
1 tablespoon fresh basil
1 tablespoon fresh oregano
3 tablespoons olive oil, divided
3/4 pound boneless, skinless chicken breasts
1/2 pound broccoli florets
1/2 pound fresh mushrooms, sliced
1 (12-inch) pre-baked pizza crust
1 tablespoon garlic salt
1 tablespoon Italian seasoning
10 ounces shredded Mozzarella cheese, divided

Sauté minced garlic, basil and oregano in 2 tablespoons of the olive oil in a skillet. Cut chicken into 1 1/2-inch pieces. Cut broccoli into bite-sized pieces. Add chicken and broccoli. Cook until chicken is no longer pink. Add mushrooms. Cook until chicken is cooked thoroughly. Drain and discard oil.

Spread the remaining 1 tablespoon olive oil on pizza crust. Sprinkle with garlic salt and Italian seasoning. Top pizza with 6 ounces of the shredded Mozzarella cheese, chicken, broccoli and mushroom mixture. Sprinkle with the remaining 4 ounces Mozzarella cheese. Bake in a preheated 400 degree oven for 10 to 12 minutes or until crust is crisp. *Yield: 4 to 6 servings*

# Tri-Color Rice Pilaf

*Great with our Grilled Swordfish with Spicy Salsa*

- 1/2 cup chopped onion
- 1 tablespoon unsalted butter
- 1 cup long grain rice (Jasmine preferred)
- 1 1/3 cups chicken broth
- 1/2 teaspoon salt
- 1/4 medium carrot, peeled
- 1/4 medium zucchini
- 1/4 medium yellow squash

Sauté onion in butter over medium heat in a saucepan until translucent. Add rice and cook for 30 seconds. Add chicken broth and salt. Boil and reduce heat to low. Cover and simmer for 13 to 15 minutes or until rice is done. While rice is cooking, julienne cut carrot, zucchini and yellow squash. Add to rice. Cover and simmer for 1 minute. Serve hot.
*Yield: 2 to 4 servings*

# Baked Wild Rice

- 1/2 cup sliced mushrooms
- 1/2 cup sliced celery
- 1/2 cup long grain wild rice
- 1/2 cup wild pecan rice
- 1 can (14 1/2 ounces) French Onion Soup
- 1 can (14 1/2 ounces) chicken broth
- 3/4 cup butter, melted
- 1 can (8 ounces) sliced water chestnuts

Combine ingredients in 9x13-inch ovenproof baking dish. Bake uncovered in a preheated 350 degree oven for 1 hour. Serve hot.
*Yield: 4 to 6 servings*

# Classic White Risotto

- 1 medium onion, minced
- 5 tablespoons unsalted butter, divided
- 2 cups Arborio rice
- 1/2 cup white wine
- 8 cups broth (chicken, beef or vegetable)
- 2/3 cup freshly grated Parmesan cheese
  salt and pepper

Cook onion slowly in 3 tablespoons of the butter over medium heat in a heavy saucepan for 8 minutes or until translucent. Do not brown onion. Stir in Arborio rice. Cook for 3 minutes or until rice appears chalky. Add white wine and cook until wine is absorbed.

Meanwhile, heat broth over medium heat in a separate saucepan to a gentle boil. Stir heated broth into rice mixture, 1 cup at a time. Each cup must be absorbed before adding another cup of broth. Stir rice continuously, or it will stick. After 6 cups of broth have been added, start adding broth in 1/2 cup increments, testing rice for tenderness. Cooked rice should be tender but firm. Remove from heat. Stir in the remaining 2 tablespoons butter and Parmesan cheese. Season with salt and pepper. Serve immediately. *Yield: 8 side servings*

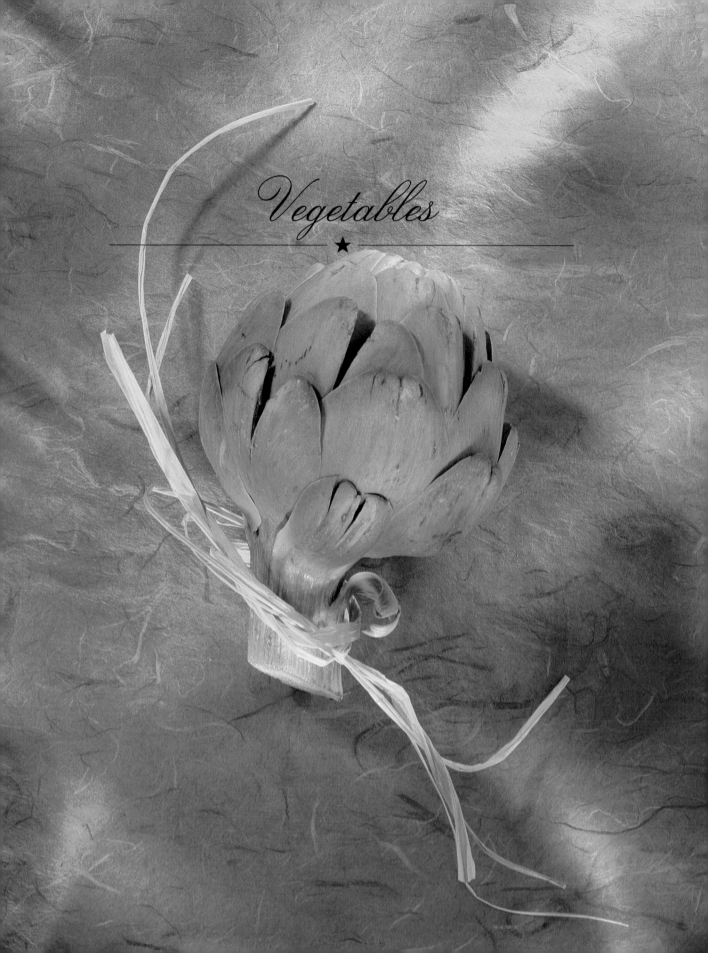

Vegetables

★

# Vegetables

★

Tomatoes Toccata.

## Tomatoes Toccata

*Excellent for a summer buffet*

8 ripe tomatoes
3/4 cup chopped fresh Italian parsley, divided
1/4 cup olive oil
2 tablespoons tarragon vinegar
2 teaspoons Dijon mustard
1 teaspoon sugar
1 clove garlic, minced
1 teaspoon salt
1/4 teaspoon pepper
8 fresh basil leaves

Cut stem ends from tomatoes. Cut vertical 1/2-inch slices into each tomato, being careful not to slice through. Stuff 1 tablespoon of the parsley between the slices of each tomato, using 1/2 cup of the parsley. Place in a shallow serving dish.

Whisk together 1/8 cup of the parsley, olive oil, vinegar, Dijon mustard, sugar, garlic, salt and pepper. Pour over tomatoes. Cover and refrigerate until ready to serve. Let stand at room temperature for 30 minutes before serving. Garnish with the remaining 1/8 cup parsley and basil leaves.
*Yield: 8 servings*

★ *Try different kinds of tomatoes for variety.*

## Spinach Ricotta Stuffed Tomatoes

*Attractive and easy*

1 package (10 ounces) frozen chopped spinach
8 ripe tomatoes
  salt
1 cup finely chopped onions
3 tablespoons olive oil
1/4 teaspoon grated nutmeg
  salt and pepper
1 cup Ricotta cheese
2 egg yolks
1/2 cup pine nuts
1/2 cup freshly grated Parmesan cheese, divided
1/2 cup chopped Italian parsley

Thaw and drain spinach. Wash and dry tomatoes. Cut off the tops and gently remove the tomato seeds and pulp. Season cavities with salt. Drain tomatoes upside down on paper towels.

Sauté onions in olive oil over low heat in a skillet for 20 minutes or until translucent. Add spinach and nutmeg. Season with salt and pepper. Cover and cook for 10 minutes.

Beat Ricotta cheese and egg yolks together in a mixing bowl. Add cooked spinach, pine nuts, 1/4 cup of the Parmesan cheese and parsley and mix well.

Blot the inside of tomatoes. Stuff tomatoes with spinach and cheese mixture. Sprinkle tomatoes with the remaining 1/4 cup Parmesan cheese. Bake in a preheated 350 degree oven for 20 minutes.
*Yield: 8 servings*

# Baked Spinach Loaf with Cheese Sauce

*Elegant and easy to prepare*

  3  packages (10 ounces) frozen chopped
     spinach
1/2  pound fresh mushrooms, sliced
1/2  cup finely chopped onions
  2  tablespoons olive oil
  6  eggs, beaten
  6  tablespoons half and half or milk
  2  teaspoons salt, divided
1/4  teaspoon grated nutmeg
1/2  cup butter
1/4  cup flour
  2  cups warm milk
  1  cup shredded Cheddar cheese

Thaw and drain spinach. Sauté mushrooms and onions in olive oil in a skillet until onions are translucent. Remove to a mixing bowl. Add spinach, eggs and half and half. Mix well. Add 1 teaspoon of the salt and nutmeg.

Grease sides and bottom of a 5x9-inch loaf pan. Line bottom with wax paper. Pour spinach mixture into loaf pan and press down well. Place pan in a large pan of hot water. Bake in a preheated 350 degree oven for 1 3/4 hours or until center is firm. Let stand for 5 minutes. Loosen loaf around sides with a knife and invert onto a serving platter. Remove wax paper.

Melt butter over low heat in a saucepan. Add flour. Stir until smooth. Add warm milk slowly. Cook sauce, stirring constantly, until thick and smooth. Add Cheddar cheese and remaining 1 teaspoon salt. Cook, stirring constantly, until cheese melts and sauce is smooth. Serve with the spinach loaf.
*Yield: 8 to 10 servings*

# Broccoli with Pine Nuts

*Delicious hot or cold*

   1  head of broccoli
1 1/2  tablespoons pine nuts
   2  tablespoons olive oil
   2  cloves garlic, minced
   3  tablespoons Italian flavored bread crumbs
   2  tablespoons freshly grated Parmesan cheese,
      divided
      dash of grated nutmeg
      salt and pepper

Cut broccoli into florets. Set aside stalks for another use. Blanch broccoli florets for 1 minute in boiling water. Rinse in a colander under cool water. Drain on paper towels and set aside.

Sauté pine nuts in olive oil over medium heat in a skillet until lightly browned. Remove and set aside. Sauté garlic in the same skillet. Add broccoli florets. Cook for 7 minutes or until liquid evaporates. Add bread crumbs, pine nuts and 1 tablespoon of the Parmesan cheese. Heat thoroughly and toss well. Season with nutmeg, salt and pepper. Top with the remaining Parmesan cheese. Serve immediately.
*Yield: 6 servings*

★ *This dish can be used as a topping for pasta.*

# Green Beans and Cashews

*Add taste and color to your table*

2 pounds fresh green beans
1 cup finely chopped onions
4 tablespoons butter, melted
3/4 cup salted cashews
   juice of 1 lemon
1/2 teaspoon chopped fresh parsley
   salt and pepper

Clean and trim green beans and break in half. Cook beans in boiling water in a saucepan over high heat for 5 to 10 minutes or until tender. Drain and rinse with cold water. Sauté onions in butter in a skillet until tender. Add green beans and cashews, and cook for 2 minutes. Add lemon juice and parsley. Season with salt and pepper. Serve warm. *Yield: 8 servings*

★ *Recipe can be halved.*

# Chinese String Beans

*Simple way to dress up green beans*

1 pound fresh green beans
2 tablespoons soy sauce
2 tablespoons water
1 teaspoon cornstarch
1 teaspoon brown sugar
1 teaspoon sesame oil
2 teaspoons vegetable oil
1 teaspoon minced garlic

Trim green beans. Steam green beans for 6 minutes or until crisp-tender. Rinse with cold water and drain. Combine soy sauce, water, cornstarch, brown sugar and sesame oil in a mixing bowl until well blended. Set aside.

   Heat vegetable oil over high heat in a large skillet. Add green beans. Stir-fry for 3 minutes or until green beans start to char in spots. Add garlic and continue stir-frying for 2 additional minutes. Add soy sauce mixture and stir constantly for 1 minute or until green beans are evenly coated and glazed. Serve immediately. *Yield: 8 servings*

# Stir-Fry Snow Peas and Peppers

*Quick, low-fat recipe*

   vegetable cooking spray
1  teaspoon dark sesame oil
1¹/₂  cups julienne-cut red pepper
¹/₂  pound snow peas, trimmed
1  clove garlic, minced
1  can (8 ounces) sliced water chestnuts, drained
¹/₄  cup water
2  teaspoons sugar
4  teaspoons soy sauce
¹/₂  teaspoon cornstarch
¹/₄  teaspoon chicken-flavored bouillon granules
   dash of pepper
1  teaspoon sesame seeds, toasted

Coat a large skillet with vegetable cooking spray. Add sesame oil. Heat over medium-high heat. Add red pepper, snow peas, garlic and water chestnuts to the hot skillet. Stir-fry for 5 minutes or until crisp-tender.

Combine water, sugar, soy sauce, cornstarch, bouillon granules and pepper in a mixing bowl. Pour over cooked vegetables, and cook, stirring constantly, for 2 minutes or until sauce thickens. Garnish with toasted sesame seeds. *Yield: 4 servings*

★  *You can use yellow or orange peppers in the spring.*

# Artichokes with Pancetta

4  large artichokes
1  lemon, juiced
6  ounces pancetta
3  tablespoons olive oil
¹/₈  teaspoon salt
¹/₂  teaspoon fresh ground pepper
¹/₂  cup dry white wine

Detach stems of artichokes. Trim and remove tough outer leaves until a central core of leaves pale at the base and green on the tip remain. Trim about 2 to 2¹/₂ inches from the top of the core, eliminating all the dark green. Cut trimmed artichokes into quarters. With a paring knife, carve away the inner choke and small curled prickly leaves. Place trimmed artichoke wedges in a bowl of cold water and lemon juice.

Cut pancetta into thin strips. Sauté in olive oil in a skillet over medium-high heat until well browned. Drain artichoke wedges. Add to pancetta along with salt and pepper. Continue cooking, turning artichokes over 2 or 3 times. Add wine and cook until wine bubbles for 1 minute. Reduce heat to medium. Cover and cook for 30 minutes or until artichokes are tender when pricked with a fork. If juices remain in the pan, uncover and increase heat. Boil until liquid evaporates. Serve immediately. *Yield: 4 to 6 servings*

★  *If large artichokes are unavailable, use 6 medium artichokes.*

## Carrot Soufflé

*A sweet carrot dish*

 2  cups diced carrots, cooked and drained
1/3  cup sugar
1/4  cup butter
 1  teaspoon vanilla extract
 2  eggs
1/2  cup milk

Blend ingredients in a blender until thick and smooth. Pour into a buttered soufflé dish. Bake in a preheated 450 degree oven for 30 minutes. Serve immediately. *Yield: 4 servings*

## Rutabaga Purée

*Even if you don't like rutabagas, you'll like this recipe*

11/2  pounds rutabagas
 1  small onion, chopped
 2  tablespoons butter
   salt and pepper
   dash of grated nutmeg

Peel and cut rutabagas into 2-inch pieces. Steam rutabagas in a pot of boiling water for 30 to 40 minutes or until tender.

    Sauté onion in butter over medium heat in a skillet until onion softens.

    Purée rutabagas and onions in a food processor until coarsely puréed. Season with salt, pepper and nutmeg. *Yield: 4 servings*

★  *This recipe tastes great with roast pork.*

## Sesame Asparagus

*A Chinese-style side dish*

1  pound fresh asparagus, trimmed
1  tablespoon peanut oil
3  tablespoons minced shallots
1  tablespoon sesame seeds
2  teaspoons soy sauce
2  dashes of dark sesame oil
   freshly ground pepper
   orange zest to garnish (optional)

Heat a skillet over medium-high heat for 2 minutes. Add peanut oil and half of the asparagus in a single layer. Cook, shaking occasionally, for 3 to 4 minutes. Turn asparagus, and cook for an additional 3 minutes or until bright green with brown spots. Add 11/2 tablespoons of the shallots and 11/2 teaspoons of the sesame seeds. Cook for 1 to 2 minutes or until the shallots are transparent. Add 1 teaspoon of the soy sauce and a dash of the sesame oil. Season with pepper. Cook for 30 seconds. Transfer to a serving platter and keep warm. Cook the remaining asparagus following the same instructions. Garnish with orange zest, if desired. *Yield: 4 servings*

★  *Asparagus also can be served at room temperature.*

Sesame Asparagus.

★

## White Beans with Garlic and Sage

*Try this recipe with grilled lamb*

1 pound Great Northern beans, dried
1 medium onion, skin removed
6 fresh sage leaves
2 cans (14 ounces) vegetable or chicken broth
8 cloves garlic, minced
1/4 cup olive oil
 salt and freshly ground pepper
2 tablespoons chopped fresh parsley

Rinse beans under running water. Place beans in a mixing bowl. Fill with cold water, covering the beans by 2 inches. Soak beans for 8 to 12 hours.

Drain soaked beans and rinse again. Combine beans, onion, sage leaves, broth and enough water to bring the liquid 1 inch above beans in an 8-quart pot. Cover and simmer for 1 hour or until beans are tender but not mushy. Drain beans and remove onion and sage leaves.

Sauté garlic in olive oil over medium heat in a skillet until golden. Season with salt. Combine garlic with beans, stirring gently to avoid breaking beans. Garnish with freshly ground pepper and parsley.
*Yield: 8 to 10 servings*

★ *For a tasty bruschetta appetizer, mash the beans slightly, and serve on toasted slices of crusty baguettes.*

## Peas and Prosciutto

*A fun way to perk up peas*

1 package (24 ounces) frozen peas or
 1 pound fresh peas
1 cup chicken broth
1 cup chopped onion
2 tablespoons olive oil
1/2 cup chopped prosciutto

Cook peas in chicken broth in a saucepan until tender. Sauté chopped onion in olive oil in a skillet until translucent. Add prosciutto and cook until thoroughly heated. Combine drained peas with cooked onion and prosciutto in a serving bowl.
*Yield: 6 servings*

★ *Crumbled cooked ham can be substituted for prosciutto.*

## Vidalia Onions au Gratin

*Excellent recipe when Vidalia onions are in season*

2 1/2 cups quartered Vidalia onions
 4 cups water
2 1/2 cups shredded Cheddar cheese, divided
1/4 cup flour
 3 tablespoons butter
 salt and pepper

Boil onions in water in a saucepan until tender. Drain and combine onions with 2 cups of the Cheddar cheese, flour and butter. Season with salt and pepper. Pour into an ovenproof baking dish. Sprinkle top with the remaining 1/2 cup Cheddar cheese. Bake in a preheated 350 degree oven for 20 to 30 minutes. *Yield: 6 to 8 servings*

# Goat Cheese Mashed Potatoes

*A new taste for an old favorite*

2 pounds russet potatoes
4 cloves garlic
  salt
1/2 to 3/4 cup heavy cream
1/2 cup butter
1/3 to 1/2 cup mild Goat cheese
  salt and pepper
1/2 cup minced green onions

Peel and cut potatoes into 2-inch pieces. Place cut potatoes and garlic in a saucepan and cover with salt water. Cook for 15 to 25 minutes or until tender. Drain and mash potatoes and garlic.

Heat heavy cream, butter and Goat cheese over low heat in a saucepan, stirring occasionally, until melted and smooth. Season with salt and pepper. Keep warm.

Beat mashed potatoes, cheese mixture and green onions in a mixing bowl with an electric mixer. Beat until potatoes are fluffy and smooth. Season with salt and pepper. Transfer to a 1-quart shallow, ovenproof baking dish. Broil under a preheated broiler for 3 to 5 minutes or until golden. *Yield: 4 to 6 servings*

★ *The potatoes may be prepared 2 days in advance and refrigerated covered. Reheat potatoes in a preheated 400 degree oven for 20 minutes.*

# Mashed Sweet Potatoes with Balsamic Vinegar

*A variation of an old favorite*

5 large sweet potatoes
2 tablespoons butter
1/8 teaspoon ground cinnamon
1/8 teaspoon grated nutmeg
1 cup milk
2 teaspoons balsamic vinegar
  salt and pepper

Bake sweet potatoes in a preheated 400 degree oven for 50 minutes or until easily pierced. Cool potatoes just enough to handle. Peel and mash sweet potatoes in a mixing bowl.

Melt butter over medium heat in a saucepan. Add cinnamon and nutmeg. Remove from heat. Stir in milk. Return to heat and boil. Add milk mixture to mashed sweet potatoes. Add balsamic vinegar. Season with salt and pepper. Serve warm.
*Yield: 4 to 6 servings*

# Sweet Potatoes with Pecan Crumble

*Great holiday dish*

5 large sweet potatoes, cooked and mashed
1 cup sugar
1/2 cup butter, melted
2 eggs
1/2 cup milk
1 teaspoon vanilla extract
1 cup packed brown sugar
1/3 cup butter, chilled
1/3 cup flour
2/3 cup chopped pecans

Combine sweet potatoes, sugar, melted butter, eggs, milk and vanilla in a mixing bowl. Pour into a 9x13-inch ovenproof baking dish. Combine brown sugar, butter, flour and chopped pecans in a mixing bowl. Sprinkle over sweet potatoes. Bake in a preheated 350 degree oven for 30 minutes. *Yield: 8 servings*

# Gourmet Potatoes

*Always good with baked ham*

6 medium white potatoes
2 cups shredded Cheddar cheese
6 tablespoons butter, divided
1 1/2 cups sour cream, room temperature
1/3 cup chopped onion
1 teaspoon salt
1/4 teaspoon pepper

Boil potatoes with skins on. Cool, peel and shred using a grater. Place Cheddar cheese and 4 tablespoons of the butter in a saucepan. Cook, stirring occasionally, over low heat until almost melted. Remove from heat. Stir in sour cream, onion, salt and pepper. Fold cheese mixture into potatoes. Pour into a greased 2-quart ovenproof baking dish. Dot with the remaining 2 tablespoons butter. Bake in a preheated 350 degree oven for 25 minutes or until golden brown. *Yield: 6 to 8 servings*

★ *Low fat Cheddar cheese and light sour cream may be substituted.*

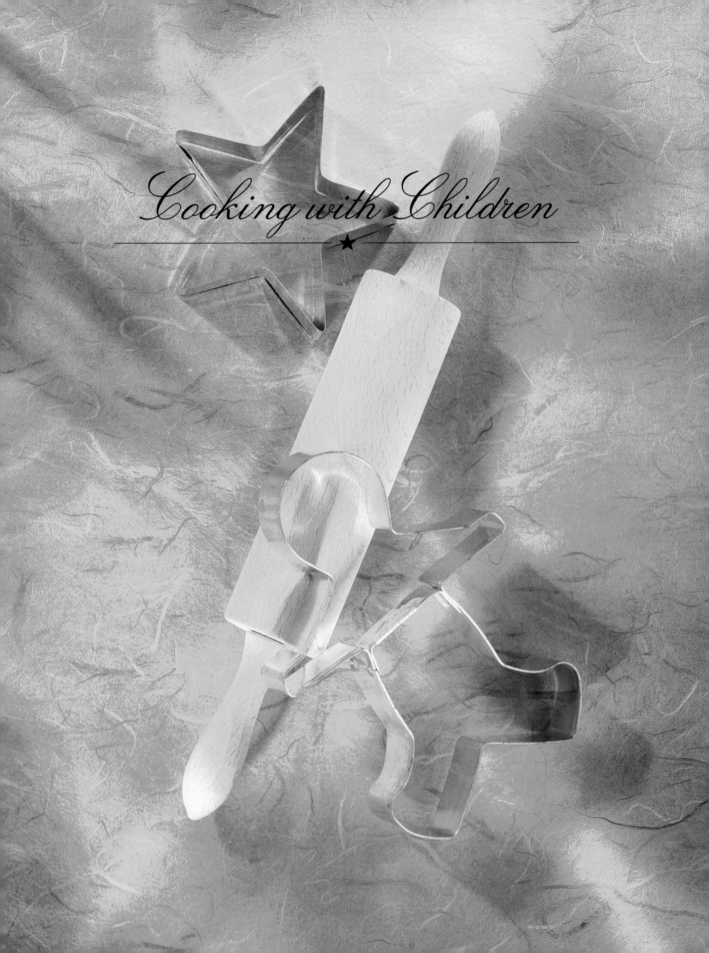

Cooking with Children

# Cooking with Children

★

Gingerbread Cookies

## Gingerbread Cookies

*Great for decorating*

- 1/2 cup unsalted butter, softened
- 1/2 cup packed brown sugar
- 1/2 cup molasses
- 1 egg
- 3 cups flour
- 3/4 teaspoon baking powder
- 1 teaspoon ground cinnamon
- 1 teaspoon ginger
- 1/4 teaspoon salt
- 1 cup confectioners' sugar
- 3 tablespoons water

Beat butter, brown sugar and molasses together with an electric mixer at high speed in a mixing bowl. Beat in egg. Mix flour, baking powder, cinnamon, ginger and salt in a separate mixing bowl. Combine flour mixture with sugar mixture. Divide cookie dough into 4 disks. Wrap each in plastic wrap. Refrigerate 2 hours or until firm. Roll 1 disk on a lightly floured surface until 1/4-inch thick. Cut rolled dough with cookie cutters. Reroll scraps, and cut more cookies. Repeat with remaining disks. Bake on an ungreased cookie sheet in a preheated 350 degree oven for 10 minutes. Cool on a wire rack.

Combine confectioners' sugar and water in a small resealable plastic bag, and knead well until smooth. Snip tip off one end of the plastic bag. Drizzle icing to decorate with dots, squiggles and swirls. *Yield: 6 dozen*

★ *Icing also can be used to affix small candies or raisins.*

## Lemon Crispies

*Great for a children's tea party*

- 1 box lemon cake mix
- 1/2 cup butter, melted
- 1 egg
- 1 cup Rice Krispies cereal

Combine cake mix, butter and egg in a mixing bowl. Gently stir in Rice Krispies. Roll dough into 1 1/2-inch balls. Place 2 inches apart on an ungreased cookie sheet. Bake in a preheated 350 degree oven for 9 minutes or until edges are golden. Cool on cookie sheet for 1 minute. Remove and cool on a wire rack. *Yield 25 to 30 cookies*

## Caramel Apple Dip

*Fun afternoon snack*

- 8 ounces cream cheese
- 1/2 cup sugar
- 1/2 cup packed brown sugar
- 1 teaspoon vanilla extract
  sliced apples

Combine cream cheese, sugar, brown sugar and vanilla with an electric mixer at high speed in a mixing bowl, scraping the sides of the bowl often, for 3 minutes or until smooth. Serve with sliced apples. *Yield: 1 cup*

★ *Dip also can be served with sliced pears.*

# Chocolate Peanut Butter Bars

*A wonderful combination*

  1 cup smooth peanut butter
  6 tablespoons butter, room temperature
1¼ cups sugar
  3 eggs
  1 teaspoon vanilla extract
  1 cup flour
¼ teaspoon salt
  2 cups semisweet chocolate chips, divided

Beat peanut butter and butter together with an electric mixer at medium speed in a mixing bowl for 1 minute or until smooth. Add sugar, eggs and vanilla. Beat until creamy. Blend in flour and salt. Stir in 1 cup of the chocolate chips. Spread cookie dough in a greased 9x13-inch ovenproof baking dish. Bake in a preheated 350 degree oven for 25 minutes or until edges brown. Remove from oven. Immediately spread the remaining 1 cup of chocolate chips on top. Let sit for 5 minutes until chocolate chips become soft and shiny. Smooth melted chocolate with a knife. Cool completely in the dish on a wire rack, and slice.
*Yield: 32 bars*

★ *Substitute chunky peanut butter for a nuttier taste.*

# Caramel Brownies

*Even adults love these brownies*

  1 box chocolate cake mix
¾ cup butter, melted
⅔ cup evaporated milk, divided
  1 bag (14 ounces) caramels
  1 cup semisweet chocolate chips

Combine cake mix, butter and ⅓ cup of the evaporated milk in a mixing bowl. Press half of cake mixture into a greased 9x13-inch ovenproof baking dish. Set aside remaining cake mixture. Bake in a preheated 350 degree oven for 10 minutes.

Melt caramels with the remaining ⅓ cup evaporated milk over medium heat in a saucepan, stirring until caramels melt. Remove cake from the oven. Sprinkle with chocolate chips. Pour melted caramel over chocolate chips. Spoon reserved cake mixture on top. Bake for an additional 20 minutes.
*Yield: 20 to 24 brownies*

★ *Children can help unwrap the caramels.*

★

## Payday Cookies

*Tastes like a candy bar*

  1  box yellow cake mix
  1  egg
3/4  cup butter, divided
  3  cups miniature marshmallows
2/3  cup light corn syrup
  2  teaspoons vanilla extract
12  ounces peanut butter chips
  2  cups Rice Krispies cereal
  2  cups salted peanuts

Combine cake mix, egg and 1/2 cup of the butter in a bowl. Pour batter into an ungreased 9x13-inch ovenproof baking dish. Bake in a preheated 350 degree oven for 12 to 15 minutes. Remove from oven. While layer is hot, sprinkle marshmallows on top.

Melt corn syrup, the remaining 1/4 cup butter, vanilla and peanut butter chips in a saucepan, stirring constantly, until smooth. Add cereal and peanuts. Mix well. Spread over top. Cool before slicing.
*Yield: 32 servings*

★ *Substitute 6 ounces of peanut butter chips with 6 ounces semisweet chocolate chips for a different taste.*

## Chocolate Chip Pizza

*Fun to make and eat*

1/2  cup sugar
1/2  cup packed dark brown sugar
1/2  cup butter, softened
  1  cup chunky peanut butter
1/2  teaspoon vanilla extract
  1  egg
1 1/2  cups flour
  1  disposable 12- or 14-inch aluminum pizza pan
  2  cups miniature marshmallows
12  ounces semisweet chocolate chips
  1  cup chopped pecans

Combine sugar, brown sugar, butter, peanut butter, vanilla and egg with an electric mixer in a mixing bowl. Add flour. Press dough into pizza pan, forming a rim around edge. Bake in a preheated 375 degree oven for 10 minutes. Remove and sprinkle with marshmallows, chocolate chips and pecans. Bake for an additional 5 minutes or until marshmallows are golden. Remove from oven, slice and cool.
*Yield: 10 servings*

★ *During the holiday season, this pizza topped with chopped candied red and green cherries or red and green "M & M's" Chocolate Candies makes a nice hostess gift.*

# Banana Bread

*Delightfully moist*

1 cup butter, softened
2 1/2 cups sugar
4 eggs, beaten
1/4 cup sour cream or yogurt
3 cups flour, unsifted
2 teaspoons baking soda
2 teaspoons vanilla extract
2 cups mashed bananas (about 4 medium bananas)

Cream butter and sugar together in a mixing bowl. Add eggs. Mix well. Add sour cream or yogurt, flour, baking soda, vanilla and bananas. Mix well. Pour batter into two 5x9-inch greased loaf pans. Bake in a preheated 350 degree oven for 45 minutes or until toothpick inserted comes out clean. *Yield: 2 loaves*

★ *Children can help peel and mash the bananas. Bananas are best when over-ripened.*

# Snowball Bread

*A sweet and sticky treat*

2 loaves frozen bread dough
3/4 cup sugar
1 tablespoon ground cinnamon
1/2 cup crushed walnuts
1/2 cup butter, melted

Thaw bread dough for 1/2 hour. Cut dough in half lengthwise. Then cut dough into 1/2-inch pieces and roll into balls. Combine sugar, cinnamon and walnuts in a mixing bowl. Dip dough balls into butter. Roll in sugar mixture. Arrange dough balls in layers in a tube or bundt pan. Let rise for 1 hour. Bake in a preheated 375 degree oven for 25 to 30 minutes. Cool for 10 minutes. Invert pan onto a serving dish. Serve hot or cold. *Yield: 8 to 10 servings*

*Wintertime at the U.S. Capitol.*

## 24-Karat Muffins

*Another fun afternoon snack*

4 cups flour
2 1/2 cups sugar
4 teaspoons baking soda
4 teaspoons ground cinnamon
1 teaspoon salt
4 cups coarsely grated carrots
1 cup raisins
1 cup chopped pecans
1 cup shredded coconut
2 tart apples, peeled and grated
6 eggs
2 cups vegetable oil
2 teaspoons vanilla extract

Combine flour, sugar, baking soda, cinnamon and salt in an extra-large mixing bowl. Stir in carrots, raisins, pecans, coconut and apples. Whisk eggs, vegetable oil and vanilla in a separate mixing bowl. Add to flour mixture. Stir until well combined. Spoon 1/3 cup of the batter into buttered muffin cups or paper-lined muffin cups, filling to the top. Bake in a preheated 350 degree oven for 30 to 35 minutes. Cool 5 minutes in pans. Finish cooling on a wire rack. *Yield: 36 large muffins*

★ *Muffins can be frozen. To simplify preparation, purchase pre-shredded carrots at a salad bar. This recipe also can be halved, and prepared in mini-muffin cups, baking for 18 to 20 minutes.*

## Blueberry Pancakes

*Great after a slumber party*

1 cup flour
2 tablespoons sugar
1 teaspoon baking soda
1/2 teaspoon baking powder
2 eggs
2 cups buttermilk
1/4 cup vegetable oil
butter or vegetable cooking spray
1 pint fresh blueberries

Combine flour, sugar, baking soda and baking powder in a mixing bowl. Whisk in eggs, buttermilk and vegetable oil. Let batter stand for 5 to 10 minutes. Spoon 1/4 cup of the batter onto a buttered, hot large skillet. Quickly drop several blueberries into each pancake by hand. Flip pancakes when bubbles on top of the batter burst. Remove to a plate when other side is brown. Serve hot with butter and syrup. *Yield: 4 servings*

★ *Try making silver dollar size pancakes.*

# Western Salad

*A teenager's delight*

1 pound ground beef
  salt and pepper
1 package ranch salad dressing mix
1 cup milk
1 cup mayonnaise
1 head green leaf lettuce, shredded
1 large avocado, diced
2 large tomatoes, diced
1/2 cup chopped onions
2 cups shredded Cheddar cheese
1 can (16 ounces) three-bean salad, drained
1/2 bag (9 ounces) nacho-flavored tortilla
  chips, crushed

Brown ground beef over medium-high heat in a skillet. Season with salt and pepper. Drain fat and cool.

Whisk together ranch salad dressing mix, milk and mayonnaise in a bowl and set aside.

Combine ground beef, ranch dressing, lettuce, avocado, tomatoes, onions, Cheddar cheese, three-bean salad and tortilla chips in a large serving bowl. Serve immediately. *Yield: 8 servings.*

★ *Add diced jalapeño peppers for kick.*

# Chicken Florentine

*Spinach will make you as strong as Popeye*

4 boneless, skinless chicken breasts
1 egg
1/3 cup dry bread crumbs
1/4 teaspoon garlic salt
  dash pepper
2 tablespoons olive oil
1 (10 ounces) package frozen chopped
  spinach, thawed and drained
1 cup shredded Mozzarella cheese

Flatten chicken breasts with a meat mallet until thin. Beat egg in a shallow bowl. Combine bread crumbs, garlic salt and pepper in a shallow bowl. Dredge chicken in beaten egg and then bread crumb mixture.

Brown chicken in olive oil in a skillet over medium-high heat for 5 minutes per side. Transfer to a greased ovenproof serving dish. Top each breast with 1/4 of the spinach and sprinkle with 1/4 of the Mozzarella cheese. Bake in a preheated 350 degree oven for 10 to 15 minutes or until juices run clear and cheese is melted. *Yield: 4 servings*

# Crescent Chicken Bundles

*Easy and attractive*

3 ounces cream cheese, softened
3 tablespoons butter, melted, divided
2 cups cubed, cooked chicken
1/4 teaspoon salt
1/3 teaspoon pepper
2 tablespoons milk
1 tablespoon chopped onion
1 tablespoon chopped chives
1 tablespoon chopped pimento or
   2 tablespoons diced red pepper
1 package (8 ounces) refrigerated
   crescent dough

Blend cream cheese and 2 tablespoons of the butter in a mixing bowl until smooth. Stir in chicken, salt, pepper, milk, onion, chives and pimento or red pepper. Separate crescent dough into four rectangles and seal perforations. Spoon 1/2 cup of the chicken mixture into center of each rectangle. Pull corners of dough over filling. Seal. Brush top with the remaining melted butter. Bake on an ungreased baking sheet in a preheated 350 degree oven for 20 to 25 minutes. *Yield: 4 servings*

★ *For variety, replace chicken filling with a mixture of 1 cup chopped cooked ham, 1/2 cup shredded Swiss cheese and 1 teaspoon prepared mustard.*

# Cap'n Crunch Chicken Fingers

*Children will flip over these*

4 boneless, skinless chicken breasts
1 1/4 cups flour, divided
1/2 teaspoon salt
1/4 teaspoon pepper
1 cup club soda
4 cups Cap'n Crunch cereal
   vegetable or canola oil

Cut each chicken breast into 6 or 7 long, thin pieces. Combine 1/2 cup of the flour, salt and pepper in a shallow bowl. Combine the remaining 3/4 cup flour and club soda in a separate shallow bowl. Crush cereal in a resealable plastic bag until fine, or process in a food processor until fine. Place crushed cereal in a third shallow bowl.

Heat 2 inches of vegetable or canola oil over medium-high heat in a skillet. Dredge each chicken piece in flour mixture, flour and club soda mixture and crushed cereal. Fry chicken pieces in hot oil for 2 to 4 minutes on each side or until golden brown. Serve hot with dipping sauces such as ranch dressing, sweet and sour sauce, or honey mustard dressing. *Yield: 24 to 28 pieces*

★ *Children can help crush the cereal. Chicken can be made ahead, and frozen for 1 month. To reheat frozen chicken pieces, bake in a preheated 350 degree oven for 10 minutes or until hot and crispy.*

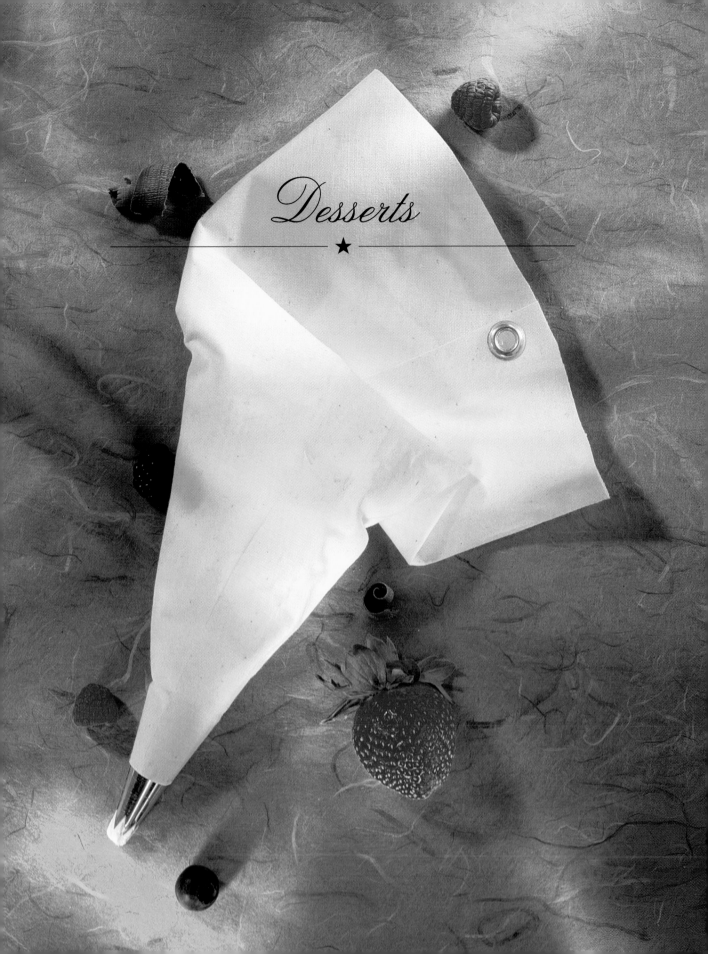

# Desserts
★

# Desserts

★

Lemon Lover's Layer Cake.

★

# Lemon Lover's Layer Cake

*A heavenly creation*

     3 cups sifted cake flour
     1 tablespoon baking powder
 1/2 teaspoon baking soda
 1/2 teaspoon salt
     1 cup unsalted butter, softened
     2 cups sugar
     1 tablespoon grated lemon zest
     4 eggs
 1 1/2 cups buttermilk
 1 1/2 teaspoons vanilla extract
     1 jar (10 ounces) lemon curd
     2 cups heavy cream
 1/4 cup confectioners' sugar
     1 cup sliced almonds, toasted

Sift flour with baking powder, baking soda and salt in a mixing bowl, and set aside. Cream butter, sugar and grated lemon zest with an electric mixer in a separate mixing bowl until pale yellow and fluffy. Beat eggs in, 1 at a time, thoroughly. With electric mixer on low, add flour mixture in thirds, alternating with buttermilk. Add vanilla, and beat until smooth. Divide batter evenly between two buttered and floured 9-inch cake pans. Bake in a preheated 350 degree oven for 30 minutes or until cakes are golden and a toothpick inserted in center comes out clean. Cool.

Remove cooled layers from the pans. Cut layers in half horizontally with a serrated knife. Spread lemon curd evenly between 4 layers, and stack on serving plate. Whip heavy cream and confectioners' sugar together. Frost sides and top with whipped cream. Cover sides and top with sliced almonds.
*Yield: 12 servings*

★ *If time permits, chill frosted cake for several hours before garnishing with toasted almonds.*

# Espresso-Hazelnut Cheesecake

*A knockout combination*

1¹/4 cups hazelnuts, toasted and skinned,
    divided
  8 ounces graham crackers
  2 tablespoons sugar
³/4 teaspoon ground cinnamon
  5 tablespoons unsalted butter, melted
  2 pounds cream cheese, softened
1¹/4 cups sugar
  4 eggs
  1 cup sour cream
¹/2 cup whipping cream, chilled
  3 tablespoons instant espresso powder
  2 tablespoons warm water
  2 teaspoons vanilla extract
²/3 cup whipping cream, chilled

Butter bottom and sides of a 9-inch springform pan. Wrap outside with double layer of aluminum foil. Coarsely process ³/4 cup of the hazelnuts in a food processor. Set aside. In same work bowl, process graham crackers, the remaining ¹/2 cup hazelnuts, sugar and cinnamon. Add melted butter. Process until crumbly. Press on bottom and sides of prepared pan. Chill.

Beat cream cheese with an electric mixer in a mixing bowl until smooth. Add sugar and eggs, 1 at a time, and beat until just blended. Add sour cream and ¹/2 cup whipping cream. Combine espresso powder and warm water in a separate mixing bowl. Combine with cream cheese filling. Add vanilla and ³/4 cup of the chopped hazelnuts.

Pour into springform pan. Place pan in a large baking pan filled halfway with hot water. Bake in a preheated 350 degree oven for 1 hour and 15 minutes or until top is puffed and center is almost set. Cool in oven with heat turned off, and oven door ajar for 1 hour. Transfer to a wire rack to finish cooling. Wrap in aluminum foil and chill overnight.

Run a knife around sides of pan to loosen cheesecake. Remove pan sides. Whip ²/3 cup whipping cream in a mixing bowl until peaks form. Spoon whipped cream into a pastry bag. Pipe around top edge and base of the cheesecake. *Yield: 14 servings*

★ *Eight ounces of graham crackers is equal to 2¹/2 cups of graham cracker crumbs.*

## Viennese Nut Torte

*Reminiscent of an Old World patisserie*

8 ounces hazelnuts or walnuts
8 eggs, separated
3/4 cup sugar
1 teaspoon baking powder
1 tablespoon fresh bread crumbs
1/2 lemon, juiced and zested

Grind nuts in a food processor. Set aside. Combine egg yolks and sugar in a mixing bowl. Beat in baking powder. Add ground nuts and bread crumbs and combine well. Add lemon juice and lemon zest.

Beat egg whites in a separate mixing bowl until they hold a firm peak. Fold egg whites gently into nut mixture until thoroughly incorporated. Pour into a springform pan. Bake in a preheated 350 degree oven for 40 minutes or until filling appears set. Serve with whipped cream or drizzle with a dark chocolate sauce. *Yield: 8 to 10 servings*

★ *For a special occasion, halve torte horizontally and fill with raspberry or apricot preserves. Cover top and sides with a dark chocolate glaze. To make glaze, bring 1 cup heavy cream to a boil. Remove from heat and stir in 9 ounces finely chopped bittersweet chocolate until melted and smooth. Garnish sides of cake with chopped nuts.*

## Coconut Pound Cake

*Coconut fans will swoon*

1 1/2 cups unsalted butter, softened
3 3/4 cups sugar, divided
6 eggs
3 cups flour
1/4 teaspoon baking soda
1 cup sour cream
1 teaspoon rum extract
1 teaspoon coconut extract
1 cup sweetened flaked coconut
3/4 cup water
1 teaspoon almond extract

Cream butter with an electric mixer in a mixing bowl. Gradually add 3 cups of the sugar at high speed. Add eggs, 1 at a time, beating well after each addition. Sift flour and baking soda in a separate mixing bowl. Add flour mixture to the butter/egg mixture alternating with sour cream, rum extract and coconut extract. Add coconut. Pour into a greased and floured 10-cup tube or bundt pan. Bake in a preheated 325 degree oven for 1 1/2 hours. Cool in pan for 10 minutes.

Boil water, the remaining 3/4 cup sugar and almond extract for 5 minutes in a saucepan. Cool slightly before using. Remove cake to a serving platter and brush with glaze. *Yield: 10 servings*

# Fudgy Brownie Cake

*An intensely chocolate cake*

1 1/2 cups unsalted butter
  6 ounces unsweetened chocolate
  3 cups sugar
  5 eggs
  1 cup walnuts, coarsely chopped
1 1/2 cups flour
1 1/2 teaspoons vanilla extract
  3/4 teaspoon salt
  3 cups whipping or heavy cream
16 ounces semisweet chocolate
  2 (1.65 ounces) milk chocolate bars

Melt butter and unsweetened chocolate over low heat in a saucepan, stirring frequently, until smooth. Remove from heat. Beat in sugar and eggs with whisk or spoon until blended. Add walnuts, flour, vanilla and salt. Mix well. Spread batter evenly in 3 greased 9-inch round cake pans lined with aluminum foil. Bake in a preheated 350 degree oven for 20 to 25 minutes or until a toothpick inserted comes out moist but not runny. Cool cakes in pans for 10 minutes. Remove aluminum foil and transfer to wire racks to continue cooling.

Heat cream and semisweet chocolate over medium heat, stirring often, in a saucepan. Boil for 1 minute. Pour chocolate cream frosting into a mixing bowl. Refrigerate, stirring once or twice, for 2 hours or until just cooled. Beat with an electric mixer at high speed until soft peaks form.

Place 1 cake layer on a serving platter. Spread 3/4 cup of the chocolate cream frosting on top. Repeat with second cake layer and 3/4 cup of the chocolate cream frosting. Top with the remaining cake layer and spread 2 cups of the frosting on top and sides. Place the remaining frosting in a decorating bag with a medium rosette tube, and decorate top and sides with chocolate rosettes. Shave milk chocolate bars into thin strips with a vegetable peeler. Sprinkle chocolate shavings on top. Refrigerate for at least 1 hour before serving. *Yield: 16 servings*

★ *Begin preparing 5 hours before serving or the day ahead. Freezes well.*

# Bananas Foster Cheesecake

*A sweet ending*

3/4 cup flour

3/4 cup finely chopped pecans

4 tablespoons unsalted butter, melted

2 tablespoons sugar

3 tablespoons brown sugar

4 1/2 teaspoons vanilla extract, divided

16 ounces cream cheese, softened

1 1/2 cups sugar, divided

2 tablespoons cornstarch

3 eggs

2 cups mashed bananas (approximately 4 bananas)

2 cups sour cream, divided

2 tablespoons fresh lemon juice

1 1/2 teaspoons ground cinnamon, divided

pinch of salt

1/2 teaspoon sugar

2 bananas

1 jar (15 ounces) caramel sauce

1/4 cup dark rum

Combine flour, pecans, butter, 2 tablespoons of the sugar, brown sugar and 2 teaspoons of the vanilla in a mixing bowl. Wrap outside of a 10-inch springform pan with aluminum foil. Press crust on bottom of pan.

Beat cream cheese with an electric mixer on medium speed until smooth. Add 1 1/4 cups of the sugar slowly. Add cornstarch. Beat eggs in, 1 at a time. Add mashed bananas. Add 1 cup of the sour cream, lemon juice, 2 teaspoons of the vanilla, 1 teaspoon of the cinnamon and salt, beating until thoroughly combined. Do not overbeat.

Pour into crust-lined pan. Place in a large baking pan filled with 1 inch hot water. Bake in a preheated 350 degree oven for 1 hour and 15 minutes or until the center is set. Remove and set aside.

Mix the remaining 1 cup sour cream, 1/4 cup sugar and 1/2 teaspoon vanilla in a mixing bowl. Spread on cooked cheesecake, and bake 10 additional minutes. Turn off oven. Cool cheesecake in oven for 2 hours or until room temperature. Refrigerate overnight or until well chilled.

Loosen cheesecake by running a knife around edges. Remove springform pan sides. Transfer to a serving plate.

Combine 1/2 teaspoon sugar and remaining 1/2 teaspoon cinnamon in a mixing bowl. Sprinkle on top of cheesecake. Peel and slice 2 bananas 1/2-inch thick. Decoratively arrange sliced bananas on top of cheesecake.

Warm caramel sauce and rum in a saucepan. Decoratively drizzle some of caramel sauce on top. Pass the remaining caramel sauce separately.

*Yield: 8 to 10 servings*

★ *Low fat sour cream and cream cheese work great in this cheesecake.*

# Tiramisù

*The Italian "pick-me-up"*

   8  egg yolks
1³/4 cups sugar
   2  cups mascarpone cheese
   2  cups heavy or whipping cream
²/3 cup boiling water
   1  tablespoon instant espresso powder
¹/4 cup coffee flavored liqueur
   3  packages (3 ounces each) ladyfingers
   2  teaspoons unsweetened cocoa powder
      chocolate curls for garnish

Combine egg yolks and sugar and whip for 1 minute or until thick and lemon colored. Place in top of double boiler over boiling water. Reduce heat to low. Cook, stirring constantly for 8 to 10 minutes or until mixture begins to thicken. Remove from heat. Add mascarpone cheese, beating well. Whip heavy cream in a separate mixing bowl until stiff peaks form. Fold into egg mixture and set aside. Stir boiling water, instant espresso and coffee liqueur in a mixing bowl. Line bottom and sides of a 10-inch springform pan with ladyfinger halves. Using a pastry brush, moisten ladyfingers with espresso mixture. Spoon half of egg yolk-cream mixture over ladyfingers and spread evenly. Repeat with ladyfingers, espresso and egg yolk-cream mixture. Dust with unsweetened cocoa powder. Garnish with chocolate curls. Cover and refrigerate overnight. To serve, unmold from springform pan and slice.
*Yield: 12 to 10 servings*

# Bittersweet Chocolate Hazelnut Torte

*Divine*

¹/4 cup hazelnuts, toasted
³/4 pound good quality bittersweet chocolate, chopped
10  tablespoons unsalted butter
¹/2 cup sugar
   6  eggs, separated
¹/4 cup flour

Grind hazelnuts in a food processor or blender. Measure out ¹/4 cup of the ground hazelnuts and set aside extra for garnish.

Melt chocolate, butter and sugar in a mixing bowl set over a pan of simmering water and set aside. Beat egg yolks in a mixing bowl for 1 minute. Add ¹/4 cup ground hazelnuts and flour. Combine melted chocolate and egg yolk/flour mixture, mixing well. Beat egg whites in a separate mixing bowl with an electric mixer until firm peaks form. Add ¹/3 of the beaten egg whites to chocolate. Fold in the remaining egg whites until thoroughly incorporated. Pour batter into a buttered 9-inch springform pan. Bake in a preheated 350 degree oven for 30 minutes. Cool. Sprinkle the reserved hazelnuts on top of torte. Serve at room temperature. *Yield: 8 to 10 servings*

# Raspberry Frangipane Tart

*Almond paste perfumes this raspberry-studded tart*

    4 ounces almond paste
 1/4 cup sugar
    2 eggs
    4 tablespoons unsalted butter, softened
 1/4 cup flour
    1 unbaked 9- or 10-inch Tart Shell
      (recipe below)
    1 pint fresh raspberries

Beat almond paste, sugar and eggs in a mixing bowl until smooth. Beat in softened butter, 1 tablespoon at a time, until well combined. Add flour with an electric mixer at low speed.

Spread filling evenly in unbaked Tart Shell. Starting from the center, arrange raspberries, right side up, on filling close to each other. Lightly press raspberries into filling. Bake in a preheated 350 degree oven for 45 minutes or until filling is set and begins to turn golden. *Yield: 8 servings*

Tart Shell
    8 tablespoons unsalted butter, chilled
    1 cup flour
    2 teaspoons sugar
 1/8 teaspoon salt
    3 tablespoons ice water

Cut butter into pieces. Process butter, flour, sugar and salt in a food processor until it resembles coarse sand. Add ice water. Pulse several times until it begins to hold together. Do not let dough form a ball. Place on a large piece of floured wax paper, pressing dough down, and shaping into a flat circle. Wrap in wax paper and chill for 30 minutes. Roll dough out on a floured surface. Transfer to a 9-inch tart pan with a removable bottom. Press dough into fluted edges of tart pan. Chill until ready to use.

# Chocolate Pine Nut Tart

*The pine nut takes center stage in this festive tart*

    4 ounces semisweet chocolate, chopped fine
    4 tablespoons unsalted butter
    1 cup dark corn syrup
 1/2 cup sugar
    3 eggs
      pinch of salt
    2 tablespoons rum or flavored liqueur
    2 cups pine nuts, lightly toasted
    1 unbaked 9- or 10-inch Tart Shell
      (recipe at left)

Melt chocolate and butter in a mixing bowl set over a pan of simmering water. Combine corn syrup and sugar over medium heat in a saucepan, bringing to a boil. Remove the saucepan from the heat. Add melted chocolate, stirring until combined. Whisk eggs, salt and rum in a separate mixing bowl. Add to chocolate mixture until just combined. Add pine nuts. Pour into unbaked Tart Shell. Bake in a preheated 350 degree oven for 40 minutes or until filling sets. *Yield: 8 servings*

★ *This unique and distant cousin of the pecan pie will appeal to pine nut and chocolate lovers alike.*

# Fresh Peach Pie with Cinnamon Ice Cream

*A summertime treat*

1 cup sour cream
3/4 cup plus 1 teaspoon sugar
4 tablespoons flour
6 to 8 fresh ripe peaches, peeled and sliced
1 (9-inch) pie crust, unbaked
1 teaspoon ground cinnamon
    Cinnamon Ice Cream (recipe at right)

Cinnamon Ice Cream
    2 cups heavy cream, divided
    2 cups milk
    1 vanilla bean
    3 sticks cinnamon
    3 egg yolks
3/4 cup sugar
    2 teaspoons ground cinnamon

Combine sour cream, 3/4 cup sugar and flour in a mixing bowl. Add sliced peaches, and gently toss by hand. Pour into unbaked pie shell. Combine 1 teaspoon sugar and cinnamon in a mixing bowl, and sprinkle on top of pie. Bake in a preheated 450 degree oven for 10 minutes. Lower the heat to 350 degrees, and bake for an additional 45 minutes. An additional 10 minutes of baking may be required if peaches are very fresh and juicy. Cool. Serve chilled or at room temperature with Cinnamon Ice Cream. *Yield: 8 servings*

Combine 1 cup of the cream with milk in a heavy saucepan. Split vanilla bean in half lengthwise. Scrape seeds into saucepan. Add vanilla bean and cinnamon sticks. Scald the mixture. Set aside. In a double boiler, whisk together egg yolks and sugar. Slowly pour in scalded milk and cream. Cook, stirring constantly, until thick enough to coat back of a spoon. Remove from heat. Remove vanilla bean and cinnamon sticks. Add the remaining 1 cup cream and ground cinnamon. Chill in refrigerator. Freeze in an ice cream maker according to manufacturer's instructions. *Yield: 1 quart*

★

## Gingered Apple Pear Crisp

*Ginger adds zing and updates a classic*

3/4 cup sugar
1 tablespoon fresh lemon juice
1/2 teaspoon ground cinnamon
1/3 cup water
6 apples
3 pears
1/4 cup crystallized ginger, finely chopped
1/2 cup unsalted butter, chilled
1 1/2 cups flour
1/4 teaspoon salt
3/4 cup packed light brown sugar

Combine sugar, lemon juice, cinnamon and water in a mixing bowl. Peel, core and thinly slice apples and pears. Toss with sugar mixture. Add ginger. Transfer to a 9x13-inch ovenproof baking dish.

Cut butter into pieces and combine with flour and salt in a mixing bowl. Add brown sugar and work mixture with fingertips until crumbly. Sprinkle evenly over fruit.

Bake in a preheated 375 degree oven for 1 hour. Serve warm or at room temperature with vanilla ice cream. *Yield: 8 servings*

## Fresh Blueberry Crumb Pie

*A delicious take on an old favorite*

1/3 cup sugar
1 1/4 cups flour, divided
1/2 teaspoon ground cinnamon
4 1/2 cups fresh blueberries
1 (9-inch) pie crust, unbaked
1 tablespoon lemon juice
1/2 cup packed dark brown sugar
1/2 cup unsalted butter, chilled

Combine sugar, 1/4 cup of the flour, cinnamon and blueberries in a mixing bowl. Pour into unbaked pie crust. Sprinkle with lemon juice.

Combine the remaining 1 cup flour and brown sugar in a mixing bowl. Cut butter in with a pastry blender or fork until it resembles coarse crumbs. Sprinkle over pie.

Bake in a preheated 425 degree oven for 30 minutes. Cover with aluminum foil. Bake for an additional 20 minutes. *Yield: 8 servings*

## Berries and Honey Cream

*Celebrate Summer with ease*

1 pint blueberries
1 pint strawberries
1 pint blackberries
8 ounces sour cream
1/4 cup honey

Wash berries. Whisk sour cream and honey together in a mixing bowl. Add more honey to taste, if desired.

Divide berries into individual serving dishes and serve with a generous dollop of honey cream. *Yield: 6 servings*

# Fruit Crumble

*Truly easier than pie*

 1  cup sugar, divided
 3  tablespoons cornstarch
 1/8 teaspoon salt
 1  egg, beaten
 1/2 teaspoon almond extract
 1/2 cup flour
 1/2 teaspoon ground ginger (optional)
 1/4 cup unsalted butter, chilled
 2  cups sliced peaches
 2  cups sliced plums
1 1/2 cups blueberries
 1/2 cup raspberries

Blend 1/2 cup of the sugar, cornstarch and salt together in a mixing bowl. Add egg and almond extract. Mix well. Combine flour, the remaining 1/2 cup sugar and ginger. Cut butter into the flour mixture with a pastry blender or fork until finely crumbled.

Place fruit in a pie dish. Pour filling over fruit. Sprinkle with crumb topping. Bake in a preheated 375 degree oven for 45 minutes. *Yield: 8 servings*

★  *Try substituting nectarines and blackberries for the peaches and raspberries.*

# Lemon Ice Cream Sans Machine

*Tart and refreshing*

 2  tablespoons freshly grated lemon zest
 9  tablespoons freshly squeezed lemon juice
 1  cup sugar
 1  cup milk
 1  cup heavy cream
 1/8 teaspoon salt

Combine lemon zest, lemon juice and sugar in a mixing bowl. Gradually stir in milk, heavy cream and salt. Pour into an 8-inch square baking pan.

Cover and freeze until solid around outside and mushy in middle. Stir well with a wooden spoon. Cover and continue to freeze until firm. Serve in scooped out lemon halves with a mint sprig.
*Yield: 3 cups*

★  *The ice cream, packed in a small metal bowl and covered airtight with plastic wrap and aluminum foil, will keep up to 1 week in the freezer. For lime ice cream, substitute lime zest and lime juice. Can also be made in an ice cream maker following manufacturer's instructions.*

# Chocolate Pots de Creme

*A sophisticated chocolate pudding*

3 egg yolks
1/3 cup sugar
  pinch of salt
1 1/4 cups milk
6 ounces bittersweet chocolate, chopped
1 teaspoon vanilla extract

Whisk egg yolks, sugar and salt in a mixing bowl until blended. Heat milk over medium heat in a saucepan until tiny bubbles form around edge of saucepan. Whisk hot milk into egg yolk mixture. Return combined mixture to saucepan and heat, stirring constantly, over medium-low heat for 3 minutes or until thickened, coating back of a spoon. Do not boil.

Remove custard from heat. Whisk in chopped chocolate and vanilla until chocolate is melted and smooth. Divide among 4 custard cups, goblets or ramekins. Cover and refrigerate overnight. Garnish with a dollop of whipped cream before serving.
*Yield: 4 servings*

# Puff Pastry Pears

*Impressive yet simple*

1 package (17 ounces) frozen puff pastry sheets
8 small, ripe pears
1/2 cup semisweet chocolate chips
4 tablespoons flour, divided
1 egg
1 tablespoon water
  raspberry or caramel sauce

Thaw puff pastry for 20 minutes. Peel pears, leaving stems intact. Using a melon baller, from bottom of pear, scoop out core and seeds, reserving cap. Fill each pear cavity with 1 tablespoon chocolate chips. Replace cap.

Dust a work surface with 2 tablespoons of the flour. Unfold each puff pastry sheet and roll out with a rolling pin. Dust with the remaining flour to prevent sticking. Cut each pastry sheet into quarters. Place a pear in center of each pastry square. Bring edges up, wrapping around pear. Leave pear stem exposed at top. Beat egg with water, and brush outside of pastry pears.

Bake on an ungreased baking sheet in a preheated 425 degree oven for 15 minutes. Reduce heat to 375 degrees and bake 5 additional minutes or until pastry is puffed and golden. Serve with warm raspberry sauce or caramel sauce. *Yield: 8 servings*

*Puff Pastry Pears.*

# Chocolate Chunk Cherry Granola Cookies

*Granola never tasted so good*

1 cup unsalted butter, softened
1 cup packed dark brown sugar
1/2 cup sugar
2 eggs
1 teaspoon vanilla extract
1 1/2 cups flour
1 teaspoon baking soda
1 teaspoon ground cinnamon
1/2 teaspoon salt
8 ounces semisweet or bittersweet chocolate
2 1/2 cups granola
1 cup dried cherries
1 cup chopped nuts (optional)

Cream butter, brown sugar and sugar in a mixing bowl until light. Beat in eggs and vanilla. Combine flour, baking soda, cinnamon and salt in a separate mixing bowl. Add to butter/sugar mixture.

Coarsely chop chocolate and add to dough. Stir in granola, cherries and nuts, mixing well. Drop teaspoonfuls of dough on a cookie sheet. Press with fingertips to flatten slightly. Bake in a preheated 350 degree oven for 12 minutes or until lightly browned. Cool on cookie sheet. Transfer to a wire rack to cool completely. *Yield: 4 dozen*

# Ultimate Lemon Bars

*Scrumptious in a picnic basket*

2 cups flour
1 cup unsalted butter, chilled
1/2 cup confectioners' sugar
4 eggs
2 cups sugar
1 teaspoon baking powder
1/2 teaspoon salt
2/3 cup fresh lemon juice
   confectioners' sugar to garnish

Combine the flour, butter and confectioners' sugar in a food processor until crumbly. Press mixture evenly into a 9x13-inch ovenproof baking dish. Bake in a preheated 350 degree oven for 25 minutes or until light golden. Remove from oven.

Beat eggs, sugar, baking powder, salt and lemon juice in a mixing bowl until smooth. Pour over crust. Bake lemon bars for an additional 15 to 20 minutes or until bubbly and light golden. Dust with confectioners' sugar. Chill overnight. Cut into diamonds or squares. *Yield: 32 bars*

★ *Squeeze approximately 5 lemons to obtain 2/3 cup fresh lemon juice.*

# Banana Fudge Walnut Brownies

*Sure to become a favorite*

1/4 cup unsalted butter
6 ounces semisweet chocolate chips
3/4 cup flour
1/2 cup sugar
1/2 cup chopped walnuts
1/3 cup mashed ripe banana
1/2 teaspoon vanilla extract
1/4 teaspoon baking powder
1/4 teaspoon salt
1 egg

Melt butter and chocolate chips over low heat in a saucepan. Beat flour, sugar, walnuts, mashed banana, vanilla, baking powder, salt and egg in a mixing bowl until combined thoroughly. Add butter/chocolate mixture. Pour into a greased 8-inch square baking pan. Bake in a preheated 350 degree oven for 30 minutes or until center is set. Cool completely. Cut into squares. *Yield: 10 servings*

★ *Use the ripest bananas you can find.*

# Macadamia Bars

*A taste of Hawaii*

1/2 cup unsalted butter, softened
1/4 cup sugar
1 cup flour
2 eggs, beaten
1/2 cup sweetened flaked coconut
1 1/2 cups packed light brown sugar
1 1/2 cups macadamia nuts, halved
2 tablespoons flour
1 1/2 teaspoons vanilla extract
1/2 teaspoon baking powder

Cream butter and sugar in a mixing bowl. Beat in flour. Press on bottom of a 9-inch square baking pan. Bake in a preheated 350 degree oven for 20 minutes.

Combine eggs, coconut, brown sugar, macadamia nuts, flour, vanilla and baking powder in a mixing bowl. Pour over hot crust, and bake an additional 20 minutes. Cool and cut into squares. *Yield: 10 servings*

★ *You can also try adding 6 ounces semisweet chocolate chips to the filling.*

★

## Raspberry Squares

*Irresistible*

1 cup unsalted butter, softened
1 cup sugar
1 egg, separated
  pinch of salt
1 teaspoon vanilla extract
2 cups flour
1 jar (12 ounces) raspberry preserves
1/2 cup chopped pecans
1 teaspoon ground cinnamon

Cream butter and sugar in a mixing bowl. Add egg yolk, salt and vanilla. Mix well. Add flour, continuing to mix well. Pat dough into a 9x13-inch ovenproof baking dish. Spread with raspberry preserves. Whip egg white in a separate mixing bowl until stiff. Spread over preserves. Top with chopped pecans and cinnamon. Bake in a preheated 350 degree oven for 25 to 30 minutes. Cut into squares when cool. *Yield: 24 servings*

★ *Apricot preserves also work well in these buttery cookies.*

## Dark Chocolate Truffles

*Contributed by Jacques Haeringer,*
*L'Auberge Chez Francois*

1/3 cup heavy whipping cream
12 ounces semisweet chocolate, divided
2 tablespoons Grand Marnier
1 cup confectioners' sugar
1 cup cocoa powder

Pour cream in a heavy bottomed saucepan. Bring to a boil over high heat and immediately reduce heat. Add 6 ounces of the chocolate, broken into small pieces. Stir constantly until chocolate is melted. Remove from heat and stir in Grand Marnier. Transfer to a mixing bowl. Refrigerate for 2 hours or until firm. Using a melon baller or teaspoon dipped in hot water, scoop 1-inch balls out of the truffle mixture onto a plate. Dust with confectioners' sugar, shape into balls and place on wax paper. Freeze for a minimum of 1 hour.

Melt the remaining 6 ounces chocolate in a double boiler, stirring occasionally. Set aside. Cover bottom of a small shallow baking pan with cocoa powder. Remove truffles from freezer and dip in melted chocolate, 1 at a time, coating all sides. Drop coated truffles into cocoa powder. Gently shake pan back and forth to powder truffles. Place truffles in a fine sieve and shake gently to remove excess cocoa powder. Place truffles in a single layer in a covered container and refrigerate. Serve at room temperature. *Yield: 24 truffles*

★ *Grand Marnier is an orange liqueur. Also try different liqueurs, such as Amaretto or Kahlúa, to flavor truffles.*

# Biscotti Cioccolato

*Perfect for dipping in coffee*

1 cup slivered almonds, toasted
1 3/4 cups flour
1 teaspoon baking soda
1/4 teaspoon salt
1/3 cup unsweetened cocoa powder
1 cup sugar
2 tablespoons instant espresso powder
4 ounces bittersweet chocolate, chopped
3 eggs
1 teaspoon vanilla extract
1 teaspoon almond extract
  vegetable cooking spray
4 ounces good quality semisweet chocolate,
  chopped

Coarsely chop almonds in a food processor. Remove chopped almonds and set aside. Combine flour, baking soda, salt, cocoa powder, sugar, espresso and bittersweet chocolate and process 20 to 30 seconds or until chocolate is finely chopped.

Beat eggs, vanilla and almond extracts in a mixing bowl with an electric mixer at medium speed until thick and pale. Pour egg mixture into food processor, and process until well incorporated. Mixture will be very stiff. Stir in chopped almonds.

Place dough on a floured surface and divide in half. Flour hands, and shape each portion into a 12-inch log. Place logs on a baking sheet coated with vegetable cooking spray. Bake biscotti logs in a preheated 300 degree oven for 50 minutes. Cool on a wire rack for 10 minutes.

Carefully cut each cooked log into 1/2-inch slices using a serrated knife. Bake sliced biscotti in a 300 degree oven for 20 additional minutes, turning biscotti over after 10 minutes. Cool on wire racks. Melt semisweet chocolate over low heat in a heavy saucepan, stirring until smooth. Dip flat edge of biscotti in melted chocolate, and cool on wax paper until chocolate is firm. Store in a plastic container for 2 to 3 weeks. *Yield: 3 dozen pieces*

## Almond Shortbread

*A rich and buttery cookie*

1½ cups whole unblanched almonds, toasted
    and cooled
1¼ cups flour
 ⅔ cup sugar
10 tablespoons unsalted butter, melted
    and cooled

Grind almonds, flour and sugar finely in a food
processor. Add butter, and process until well
combined. Divide dough in half, and press onto
bottom of 2 buttered 9-inch baking pans. Score
dough with a sharp knife into 16 wedge-shaped
cookies. Bake in a preheated 350 degree oven for 25
minutes or until light brown. To remove, place a
small plate on surface of shortbread, and carefully
invert onto the plate. Cool on wire racks.
*Yield: 32 cookies*

★ *The shortbread is fragile, so take care when
unmolding. Otherwise, it's a snap to prepare.*

## Poppy Seed Almond Cookies

*A perfect accompaniment to tea*

 1 cup sugar
⅓ cup unsalted butter, softened
 2 tablespoons light corn syrup
1½ teaspoons almond extract
 1 egg
 1 egg white
2¼ cups flour
 2 tablespoons poppy seeds
 1 teaspoon baking soda
    vegetable cooking spray

Cream sugar and butter with an electric mixer at
medium speed in a mixing bowl for 3 minutes or
until fluffy. Beat in corn syrup, almond extract, egg
and egg white. Combine flour, poppy seeds and
baking soda in a separate mixing bowl. Beat dry
ingredients into creamed sugar/butter until well
blended.

Drop cookie dough, by rounded tablespoons,
onto a cookie sheet coated with vegetable cooking
spray. Flatten cookies with fingertips. Bake in a
preheated 350 degree oven for 10 minutes or until
light brown. Cool on cookie sheet for 1 minute.
Transfer to wire racks to cool completely.
*Yield: 3 dozen cookies*

# Pumpkin Flan

*A new Thanksgiving tradition*

1¼ cups sugar, divided
½ teaspoon salt
1½ teaspoons vanilla extract
1 teaspoon ground cinnamon
⅛ teaspoon grated nutmeg
1 cup pumpkin filling
5 eggs
1 can (12 ounces) evaporated milk
1 cup whipping cream, whipped

Caramelize ½ cup of the sugar over low heat in a heavy saucepan. Pour into a 9- or 10-inch pie pan. Combine the remaining ¾ cup sugar, salt, vanilla, cinnamon and nutmeg in a mixing bowl. Beat in pumpkin filling, eggs and evaporated milk. Pour into pie pan. Set pie pan in a large pan filled with 1 inch of boiling water. Be careful not to get water into flan. Bake in a preheated 350 degree oven for 20 minutes. Run a knife along edge of pan. Invert onto a serving dish. Serve with whipped cream. *Yield: 8 servings*

# Creme Caramel

*A fabulous rendition of this famed custard*

4 cups sugar, divided
1½ quarts milk
10 eggs
¼ teaspoon salt
1 tablespoon vanilla extract
1 teaspoon almond extract

Caramelize 3 cups of the sugar over low-medium heat, stirring frequently, in a heavy large skillet. Sugar will start to liquefy and turn caramel golden in color. Warm a bundt or tube pan in a preheated 325 degree oven for 3 to 5 minutes while making caramel. This prevents caramel from cracking when poured into pan. Pour caramel into pan, swirling to coat all sides. Be careful because pan will become hot.

Scald milk over medium heat in a saucepan. Cool slightly. Beat eggs, remaining 1 cup sugar, salt, vanilla and almond extracts in a mixing bowl. Gradually add, stirring constantly, egg mixture to scalded milk. Pour custard mixture into caramelized pan. Place pan in a baking pan ½ filled with boiling water.

Bake in a preheated 325 degree oven for 1½ hours. Remove from oven. Refrigerate for several hours before serving or up to 1 week. When ready to serve, place a serving dish over top of pan and invert. Serve with extra caramel sauce ladled on top. *Yield: 12 to 16 servings*

# Sourdough Bread Pudding with Bourbon Sauce

*Down home flavor*

1/2 cup golden raisins
2 tablespoons Bourbon
2 cups sugar, plus extra to coat the ramekins
2 cups milk
2 cups heavy cream
1 pound day-old sourdough bread, cut into 1-inch cubes
3 eggs, beaten
3 tablespoons unsalted butter, melted
2 tablespoons vanilla extract
1/2 teaspoon ground cinnamon
Bourbon Sauce (recipe at right)

Soak raisins in Bourbon for 20 minutes. Butter 12 ramekins and dust with sugar. Pour milk and heavy cream over bread cubes in a mixing bowl. Soak for 5 minutes. Whisk eggs, 2 cups sugar, melted butter, vanilla and cinnamon together in a mixing bowl. Pour egg mixture over the bread cubes. Add raisins and toss to mix.

Spoon bread pudding into prepared ramekins. Bake in a preheated 325 degree oven for 1 hour or until golden brown. To serve, loosen pudding from the sides of ramekin with a knife, and invert onto a dessert plate. Spoon Bourbon Sauce on top.
*Yield: 12 servings*

Bourbon Sauce
1/2 cup unsalted butter
1/2 cup packed light brown sugar
1/2 cup sugar
1 egg
3 tablespoons Bourbon

Melt butter, brown sugar and sugar over low heat in a saucepan until sugars dissolve. Whisk egg in a mixing bowl. Whisk some of the melted butter/sugar mixture into beaten egg. Then combine with the remaining melted butter/sugar mixture in saucepan. Continue whisking until sauce is smooth. Do not boil. Whisk in Bourbon. *Yield: 3/4 cup*

# Cookbook Committee

★

## EDITORIAL BOARD

**Deané Fenstermaker,**
*Chair*

**Julia Ann Lake,**
*Editor In Chief*

**Emily Sawyer Jones,**
*Design Editor*

**Veronica M. De Nardo,**
*Managing Editor*

**Tracy Shipman Piper,**
*Marketing Co-Editor*

**Helen Robertson Rivers,**
*Marketing Co-Editor*

**Demetra Economos Anas,**
*Senior Food Editor*

*Chapter Food Editors*

**Maurye McCarthy,**
*Appetizers*
**Nicole Barranco,**
**Katherine Crouse,**
*Brunch and Breads*
**Kimberly Harter,**
*Salads*
**Tammy Schuette,**
*Soups*
**Elizabeth Lawson,**
*Poultry and Meats*
**Joni Chizzonite,**
*Vegetables*
**Lee Wollman,**
*Seafood*
**Deirdre Parker,**
*Pasta and Pizza*
**Shelley Church Rodgers,**
*Cooking with Children*
**Joanne Kelley Fillion,**
*Desserts*
**Janet Bertin,**
*Crowd Recipes*

## ACTIVE COOKBOOK COMMITTEE

Barbara Angel
Christina Bartley
Briana Powers Bayer
Valerie Bayle
Marjorie Best
Anne Bondelie
Audrey Charlson
Sarah Conrad
Barrie Conway
Cecily Crandall
Lisa Derby
Amy Draper
Karen T. Garre
Alisa Gooch
Angela Green
Susan B. Greer
Tina Hamlin
Joanne Heininger
Melissa Held
Mary Wall Hood
Maura Hubach
Anne Beverly Jones
Nora Keating
Natalie Kirschner
Catherine Klein
Laura Koehne
Charlotte Lekakos
Peg Luce
Claire Sechler Merkel
Margaret Pulsifer
Cynthia Raiford
Betty Sayler
Anne Sydnor
Lesly Toohey
Anne Tuccillo
Elizabeth Vick-Kabbani
Victoria Woolard
Patricia Wright

## PROVISIONAL COOKBOOK COMMITTEE

Katy Anderson
Jennifer Ballman
Kate Bannan
Beverly Barr
Maggie Basile
Stacey Garnett
Brahmey
Cindy Bucco
Joyce Brayboy Dalton
Christina Dickie
Erin Donovan
Stephanie Fretwell
Kristy Galvan
Krissy Ganong
Charlotte Giddings
Lenore B. Hall
Carolyn Hensarling
Lee Johanson
Linda Jordan
Kimberly Kelley
April Kinne
Sally Kramer
Audrey Lamb
Marilyn Lewis
Elizabeth Look
Katherine Matthews
Melissa McKee
Erin Mooney
Sue Moore
Elissa Morrison
Britt Moses
Hilary Newlin
Joyce O'Donnell
Beverly Patton
Beth Persons
Sarah Price
Melanie Ray
Artis Richardson
Fran Scofield
Nan Senter
Eleanor Shanahan
Beth Silipigni

Susan Skelton
Keili Phelan Smith
Liz Soza
Georgia E. Trapp
Kristin Walberg
Christine Waldmann
Alexandra Walge

## SUSTAINER TESTERS

Marcia Ball
Ellen Calvin
Mary Anne Clancy
Jo Ann Coleman
Ann Fagale
Mary Ellen Fahy
Judy Fitzsimmons
Diane Forestell
Linda Harrison
Kay Hobson
Patricia Mayo
Susan McCreary
Ellen Spencer
Carol Steuart
Ellen Talbott
Cynthia Toussaint
Edie Wingate

# Acknowledgements

★

## A Special Thanks To:

**Neal Cormon,**
*Blue Point Grille and Sutton Place Gourmet*

**Jacques Haeringer,**
*L'Auberge Chez Francois*

**Judy Harris,**
*Judy Harris Cooking School*

**William Jackson,**
*Carlyle Grand Cafe*

**Robert Kinkead,**
*Kinkead's*

**Carmine Marzano,**
*Luigino*

**Robert McGowan,**
*Old Ebbitt Grill*

**Mark Miller,**
*Red Sage*

**Jim Petrillo,**
*Red Sage*

**Nora Pouillon,**
*Restaurant Nora and Asia Organic Cuisine*

**Martin Saylor,**
*The Hay-Adams*

**Hidemasa Yamamoto,**
*The Jockey Club*

**Mount Vernon Ladies' Association**

**Monticello, Research Center**

*Capital Celebrations* would like to thank the many individuals who have shared with us their insights and experiences.

## Recipe Contributors

Demetra Economos Anas
Reta Anas
Colleen Aycock
Jennifer Ballman
Ann Bambrick
Cicely Banfield
Claudia Barnes
Nicole Barranco
Lisa Barrett
Christina Bartley
Briana Powers Bayer
Emily Bayle
Janet Beckmann
Beth Bolen
Ana Boudreau
Sara Boyan
Midge Bradford
Stacey Garnett Brahmey
E. Brooke Brinkerhoff
Kristyn Burnett
Natalie Bush
Susan Cambon
Susan Cantrell
Dorothy Carroll
Judy Casso
Helen Chaikosky
Gail Charnley
Joni Chizzonite
Sarah Conrad
Gigi Corbin
Cecily Crandall
Katherine Crouse
Joyce Brayboy Dalton
Fernanda Dau
Dawne D. Davis
Margeurite T. De Nardo
Veronica M. De Nardo
Vasiliki Dell'Acqua
Lisa Derby
Susan DiLiddo
Rosemary Dircks
Brenda Dolan
Amy Draper
Nathina Droussiotis
Linda DuRoss
Norma Dugger
Alleyne Easton
Stavroula Economos
Thomas Erickson
Joann Fallon
Melissa Feld
David Fenstermaker

Deané Fenstermaker
Maude Fenstermaker
Julia Fermoile
Helen Fillion
Joanne Kelley Fillion
Roger Fillion
Linda Finkelstein
C.J. Fischer
Vicki Fisk
Judy Fitzsimmons
Irene Fotos
Laura Foy
Ann Fragala
Carol Froeb
Barbara Gahagan
Karen T. Garre
Mary Garver
Wendy Gasch
Marianne Gingrich
Alisa Gooch
Angie Green
Susan B. Greer
Chris Guttierez
Lenore B. Hall
Holly Hamilton
Tina Hamlin
Betsy Hannah
DeLisa Lou Harmon
Linda Harrison
Kimberly Harter
Katherine Haw
Charlotte Hayden
Joanne Heininger
Michele Hemingway
Carolyn Hensarling
Lisa Gadra Henschel
Shannon Hobbs
Tricia Hollis
Mary Wall Hood
Caroline Hume
Susie Hurd
Anne Johns
Themis Johnson
Anne Beverly Jones
Emily Sawyer Jones
Mary Ruth Jones
Nancy Judy
Margaret Kinsey
Catherine Klein
Tuke Klemmt
Elaine Koehne
Laura Koehne

Wendy Koweynia
Julia Ann Lake
Winona Lake
Sue Landa
Susan Legg
Anne Link
Amy Littlefield
Sharon H. Longabaugh
Elizabeth Look
Heidi Mahloch
Maria Maries
Kelly Marple
Joyce L. Martin
Carmine Marzano
Katherine Matthews
Charlotte Mayden
Maurye McCarthy
Shanah McClure
Joanna McIntosh
Melissa McKee
Ann McLaughlin
Mary Clare Meade
Claire Sechler Merkel
Jennifer Miller
Janene Mitchell
Alison Mize
Mary Monahan
Janet Monroe
Erin Moss
Ann Murtlow
Gretchen Noyes
Susan O'Connell
Bonnie O'Dell
Jennifer Oldham
Cathy Orr
Deirdre Parker
Monica Petrick
Jeneva Pickett
Hildy Plante
Robin Poderski
Marlisa Post
Susan Pries
Margaret Pulsifer
Marilyn Quayle
DeDe Ralston
Henrietta Randolph
Edith Rands
Melanie Ray
Ashley Rehr
Neil Reiter
Helen Robertson Rivers
Ann Robertson

Matilda Robertson
Shelley Church Rodgers
Janet Roell
Mary Ellen Rogers
Gwen Rosenthal
Diane Rothman
Lee Royen
Mary Savino
Katherine Sawyer
Betty Sayler
Mary Frances Schorr
Serena Schorr
Tammy Schuette
Ellen Sell
Jane Sewell
Susan Skelton
Gayle Smith
Keili Phelan Smith
Regina Smith
Jill Snow
Anne Somerville
Dorothy Spence
Ellen Spencer
Anne Sydnor
Ellen Talbott
Hans Tallis
Frank Tax
Lisa Toohey
Anthony Tracanna
Georgia E. Trapp
Ann Tuccillo
Lisa Turner
Topper Vick-Kabbani
Joy Vige
Kristin Walberg
Alma Ward
Sam Warrick
Dawn Waters
Gwen Waters
Merrill Wegner
Ann Weir
Pam Whitfield
Barb Wickman
Jane Wiseman
Alexandria Wollman
Vikki Woolard
Carrie Wosicki
Pattie N. Wright
Lisa Zingone
Diane Zutant

# Index